UNDERDEVELOPMENT AND DEVELOPMENT IN BRAZIL

Vol. II: Reassessing the Obstacles to Economic Development

OTHER BOOKS BY THE AUTHOR

The Brazilian Capital Goods Industry, 1929–1964 (1968)

Economic Policy-Making and Development in Brazil, 1947–1964 (1968)

Underdevelopment and Development
in Brazil

Vol. II: Reassessing the Obstacles to Economic Development

NATHANIEL H. LEFF

London
GEORGE ALLEN & UNWIN
Boston   Sydney

George Allen & Unwin (Publishers) Ltd,
40 Museum Street, London WC1A 1LU, UK

George Allen & Unwin (Publishers) Ltd,
Park Lane, Hemel Hempstead, Herts HP2 4TE, UK

Allen & Unwin Inc.,
9 Winchester Terrace, Winchester, Mass 01890, USA

George Allen & Unwin Australia Pty Ltd,
8 Napier Street, North Sydney, NSW 2060, Australia

First published in 1982

British Library Cataloguing in Publication Data

Leff, Nathaniel H.
    Underdevelopment and development in Brazil.
Vol. 2: Reassessing the obstacles to economic development
1. Brazil – Economic conditions – History
I. Title
330.981   HC187
ISBN 0-04-330325-0

Library of Congress Cataloging in Publication Data

Leff, Nathaniel H.
    Underdevelopment and development in Brazil.
Contents: v. 1. Economic structure and change, 1822–1947 – v.2.
Reassessing the obstacles to economic development.
1. Brazil – Economic conditions. 2. Brazil – Economic policy. I. Title.
HC187.L5238   330.981   82-4026
ISBN 0-04-330324-2 (v. 1)   AACR2
ISBN 0-04-330325-0 (v. 2)

Set in 10 on 11 point Times by Bedford Typesetters Ltd,
and printed in Great Britain
by Billing & Sons Ltd, Guildford, London & Worcester

*To The Memory
of
Louis Leff*

Why did the United States industrialize in the nineteenth century, keeping pace with the nations of Europe, while Brazil in the nineteenth century evolved in the direction of transforming itself into a large underdeveloped region.

Overcoming the superstitious fatalism of the theories of climatic or "racial" inferiority, this question takes on a greater significance from an economic point of view. It seems appropriate, therefore, that we give this question some attention.

Celso Furtado, *Formação Econômica do Brasil*

Acknowledgments

Over the years in which I have worked on this study, many people have provided useful suggestions. I thank all of them; and especially Patricia Aufderheida, Richard Bird, Stephen De Canio, Michael Edelstein, Stanley Engerman, David Felix, Stefano Fenoaltea, Albert Fishlow, Richard Graham, and Herbert Klein for their comments on penultimate drafts. I am grateful to the late, lamented John Millar for his able research assistance. Nicholas Brealey of George Allen and Unwin has been an innovative editor. I am also grateful to Rowena Friedman for her care in preparing the manuscript for typesetting. Avraham Leff provided important help at a key juncture. Needless to say, none of these people bears any responsibility for deficiencies in the study.

Parts of this book appeared in a much earlier form in *The Quarterly Journal of Economics* (1972) and *The Economic History Review* (1972). I have revised and developed those materials in the light of data and analysis which have since become available. However, I am also grateful to the editors of those journals for permission to draw upon the earlier articles.

I am glad for the opportunity to thank the Faculty Research Program of the Columbia Business School for financial support. Also, this book would probably not have been written had it not been for the intellectual stimulus and support of Columbia University's Seminar in Economic History and Columbia's Latin American Institute. Finally, and as always, I am grateful to Judith for helping to make everything possible.

Contents

List of Tables

1

Introduction

This book is the companion to Volume I of *Underdevelopment and Development in Brazil*, entitled *Economic Structure and Change, 1822–1947.*[1] That study sought to clarify the central features of Brazil's economic experience between the advent of formal political independence and the country's notable economic expansion during the post-Second World War period. Elucidation of those topics raised analytical questions which could not be addressed within the length of the earlier work. The present study focuses on those issues.

More particularly, during most of the nineteenth century, the pace of economic development and per capita income growth in Brazil was relatively slow. The rate of change rose sharply toward the end of the century, however; and thereafter, Brazil was launched on a path of accelerated economic expansion and structural change. Two questions come immediately to mind. First, what were the underlying conditions which prevented Brazil from achieving more rapid economic development during most of the nineteenth century? Second, what forces finally operated which enabled the country to overcome these barriers and make the transition to sustained economic growth and structural change?

Conditions which prevent an underdeveloped country from achieving rapid economic progress may be termed obstacles to development.[2] Such obstacles may stem from non-economic realms (e.g. political or cultural conditions) as well as from directly economic behavior. In the specific context of nineteenth-century Brazil, numerous obstacles might in principle have acted to impede the country's economic development. Among those which have been proposed are: unfavorable sociocultural conditions; international imperialism; and/or the internal politics of domination by a landowner oligarchy. The list of potential catalysts is smaller. But the possible role of the Brazilian state in promoting the country's economic development surely requires attention. These topics are the subject of the work which follows.

Our list of possible obstacles to economic development in nineteenth-century Brazil may strike some readers as either too long or too short. Interpretation of Brazil's economic history is a subject which has evoked many different hypotheses. Further, a view which some readers consider self-evidently true may strike other observers as too farfetched to warrant serious discussion. Such diversity in historiographical assumptions raises obvious problems for an author who seeks to give a balanced treatment. This is, of course, the classical question of determining the relevant research agenda. I have addressed it by taking an eclectic approach, and considering a variety of interpretations. This approach also offers an additional advantage. Perceptions of what constitutes a self-evident truth for historians (and economists) have been known to change; and one generation's universally-rejected interpretation can be the basis for another generation's revisionism. But the choice of hypotheses considered here is certainly not exhaustive. The chapters presented below attempt to make some analytical progress in Brazilian economic historiography. Hopefully, the perspectives they unfold will also stimulate further research on subjects which I have omitted.

One purpose of this study, then, is to achieve a better understanding of Brazil's economic past. The book also has another objective, of wider relevance. Economists and other social scientists have devoted considerable effort to attempts at explaining the phenomenon of economic underdevelopment. One approach has been to propose various obstacles which might prevent a country from attaining long-term economic advance. These obstacles are usually plausible in *a priori* terms. They may also fit a casual empirical view of specific instances of economic underdevelopment. But discussions at that level have not led to notable insights into the causes of economic underdevelopment and development. We may achieve greater understanding if these theories of underdevelopment are confronted in a more sustained manner with actual cases of economic retardation and subsequent development.

That is the approach followed here. It offers the usual advantages present in maintaining a close interaction between social-science theory and human experience. There may also be analytical gains to including the Brazilian experience in the empirical base which social scientists consider relevant in deriving their theoretical generalizations. Special advantages accrue in this instance because our study focuses on a case which encompasses backwardness *and* later development. It would of course be intellectually gratifying if changes in the conditions noted earlier as the relevant constraint on the country's development could also be identified as the shift which launched Brazil on its new economic trajectory.

Finally, a consideration of the obstacles to economic development in this historical case also serves another purpose. Our discussion leads to conclusions not only about the conditions which appear to have restricted the pace of economic development in nineteenth-century Brazil, but also about those conditions which were not major barriers. The latter may be called 'non-obstacles', with corresponding implications concerning their importance. This study, however, aims at more than simply distinguishing the serious from the less serious (or non-operative) obstacles to Brazil's economic progress during the nineteenth century. Far more importantly, the discussion focuses on issues which are of key importance for understanding both economic development and Brazil's economic history. This perspective also provides the opportunity for systematic consideration of some questions which may have previously received insufficient analytical attention in discussions of Brazil's economic past.

As already mentioned, this study follows an earlier work, *Economic Structure and Change, 1822–1947* which provides substantive background as well as much of the statistical data that are utilized in this study. Nevertheless, the two books deal with different questions, and can certainly be read independently. In one important respect, however, the present study does draw directly on material presented in the earlier book. Research on the economic history of an underdeveloped country like nineteenth-century Brazil raises some serious methodological issues. These include the desirability of drawing useable numerical conclusions from data whose accuracy is questionable, and the question of whether meaningful research can be done on the history of countries for which some basic primary and secondary materials are often not available. Those issues are discussed in Chapter 1 of *Economic Structure*, and the interested reader is referred to that discussion.

We will begin our substantive discussion here by considering the economic history of Brazil's Northeast region during the nineteenth century. That large region had an especially poor development experience during the century; and a consideration of the Northeast's experience enables us to focus on many of the analytical issues raised in a discussion of the obstacles to Brazilian economic development. To what extent can an explanation for slow economic development be found in Brazil's social structure and cultural norms? What role did expanding foreign trade and involvement in the international economy play as an obstacle to development? And what were the effects of Brazil's political system in impeding and/or promoting economic development? The next chapter considers these issues in the context of the Northeast.

Notes

1 Nathaniel H. Leff, *Underdevelopment and Development in Brazil*, Vol. I: *Economic Structure and Change, 1822–1947* (London: Allen & Unwin, 1982).

2 For a thoughtful discussion of the notion of obstacles or 'prerequisites' to development, see Albert O. Hirschman, 'Obstacles to Development: A Classification and a Quasi-Vanishing Act,' reprinted in his *A Bias for Hope* (New Haven: Yale University Press, 1971), pp. 312–27. As in that essay, the perspective followed here is that conditions must be viewed in their specific historical context before they can be labeled obstacles or non-obstacles.

2

The Northeast and the Obstacles to Economic Development in Nineteenth-Century Brazil

Introduction

During the nineteenth century the growth of per capita income in Brazil's large Northeast region was particularly slow; and the region also lagged in overall economic development.[1] A large fraction of Brazil's total population resided in the Northeast throughout this period – approximately 52 percent in 1823, 47 percent in 1872, and 42 percent in 1890. Consequently, the Northeast's poor economic experience was of central importance in Brazil's aggregate economic retardation during the nineteenth century. In addition to the intrinsic interest in understanding why the Northeast did relatively poorly in economic terms, there is also another reason for giving particular attention to this case. A study of the Northeast's experience highlights many of the analytical issues involved in an effort to understand the obstacles to development in nineteenth-century Brazil.

The reasons for the Northeast's poor development experience during the nineteenth century are not immediately obvious. Indeed, the Northeast's failure to develop over this long period may appear especially puzzling because Brazil's other major region, the Southeast (Rio de Janeiro and São Paulo), was achieving a degree of economic progress. The question of the Northeast's poor experience during the nineteenth century also has wider ramifications. Coming in conjunction with the economic expansion of the Southeast coffee region, the Northeast's modest growth led to the emergence of a significant degree of regional inequality in Brazilian development. The meager increase of per capita income in the Northeast during the nineteenth century, and the ensuing low absolute income levels in the region also had important consequences for the Brazilian economy in the twentieth century.[2]

An analysis of the Northeast's failure to achieve significant economic development during the nineteenth century is also relevant in a broader context. The existence of regional inequalities in the process of economic development has often been noted, and various theories have been proposed to explain this phenomenon.[3] For lack of historical analysis, however, the empirical relevance of these theories is not clear.[4] Thus it is not always known whether such inequalities are generated by possible endogenous features of the development process such as the 'backwash effects' which Gunnar Myrdal has proposed; or whether regional disparities are essentially the result of a cumulative increase in a per capita income differential which prevailed before the onset of modern development; or whether regional inequalities stem from other processes which have been neglected in the theoretical literature. An historical analysis of the Brazilian experience, which is often considered a classic case of regional inequality in the development process, can clarify some of these issues.

Finally, a consideration of regional inequality in economic development is also relevant for another reason. Because of concern for equality in the development process, considerable attention has focused on the functional and on the size distributions of income. In many countries, however, much of the variance in income levels reflects wide disparities in *interregional* levels of per capita income and development. Hence a special interest attaches to the emergence of such differentials in the development process. Both for reasons related to Brazil's economic history and for reasons of general import, then, an analysis of the Northeast's poor experience during the nineteenth century would be helpful. That is the purpose of the present chapter.

Emergence of The Disparity

The Northeast–Southeast economic differential is not the result of changes which occurred in Brazil during the twentieth century. Rather, the disparity seems to have appeared toward the middle of the nineteenth century. At the beginning of the nineteenth century, the Northeast had not been a backward region within Brazil. On the contrary, the Northeast's share in the country's total export earnings seems to have been at least as high as the region's share in the total population.[5] Indeed, a leading Brazilian economic historian, Roberto Simonsen, speaks of the Southeast as having been in deep economic crisis at that time.[6] By mid-century, however, levels of per capita income seem to have been higher in the Southeast than in the Northeast.

Information on regional slave importations from Africa suggest that during the second quarter of the nineteenth century, economic expansion proceeded more rapidly in the Southeast. Thus between 1821 and 1843 some 73 percent of the slaves imported to Brazil were brought to the Southeast rather than to ports in the Northeast.[7] The Southeast's differentially higher importation occurred even though the

Northeast began the period with a much larger share of Brazil's total slave-labor force.[8] Thus the Northeast's replacement needs in the face of the poor demographic conditions of Brazil's slave population were larger than those of the Southeast. Slaves were a major component of 'capital formation' in nineteenth-century Brazil. Hence the greater net importation of slaves to the Southeast suggests a higher rate of net investment and output growth in that region. By 1845–46, the Southeast accounted for some 56 percent of the Brazilian government's revenues; the Northeast, only 31 percent.[9] This disparity occurred at a time when perhaps half of the country's population was located in the Northeast.

Evidence of a shift in relative levels of per capita output as between regions also comes from a non-conventional source – information on a reallocation of the slave-labor force within Brazil. After 1852, overseas importation of slaves to Brazil was stopped; and as a result, the country's stock of slaves was relatively fixed in the short term. Possession of slaves within Brazil remained legal, however, until 1888. What is relevant in the present context is the fact that between 1852 and 1888, the planters of the Southeast were able to bid away a sizable fraction of the Northeast's slave-labor force.[10] Since slaves were an important 'capital good' in this economy, the interregional movement of slaves reflects regional differences not only in the productivity of labor, but also in the productivity of capital. That is, the Southeast's capacity to pay higher prices for slaves indicates that the joint marginal value-product of labor and of capital was higher in that region than in the Northeast. Differences in the productivity of labor and of capital are of course an important indicator of differences in the level of per capita output. In reflection of the greater factor productivity prevailing in the Southeast, the movement of slaves from the Northeast which began in the 1850s occurred despite the existence of high interregional transportation costs. And the flow of slaves to the Southeast continued despite the subsequent imposition of taxes on interregional slave sales. By the time slavery was abolished in Brazil, approximately 75 percent of the country's slave population was concentrated in the Southeast.[11]

Other information also suggests that higher levels of per capita output and income in the Southeast date well back into the nineteenth century. Thus when large-scale European immigration to Brazil began, the immigrants were attracted mainly to the Southeast.[12] The vastly greater success of São Paulo and Rio de Janeiro in drawing European immigrants has sometimes been attributed to the region's greater promotional efforts. But it is unlikely that the Southeast could have continued to attract (and retain) a differentially larger flow of immigrants unless that region had also offered better economic opportunities than the Northeast. The declining relative attractiveness of the Northeast is also indicated by the fall in the percentage of foreign-born people in the population of the region's largest city, Recife. The percentage fell from some 20 percent in 1790–1806, to 12 percent in 1853–60, and 3 percent in 1901–10.[13] The decline in the second half of the century is especially noteworthy, for it occurred in the midst of a sharp upsurge in overall immigration to Brazil.

The opening of a significant regional income differential during the nineteenth century implies that per capita income in the Northeast grew at a rate markedly lower than in the Southeast. Why this was so is the question that will occupy us in the remainder of this chapter.

Regional Differences in Export Growth

A relatively low rate of economic growth in the Northeast during the nineteenth century has sometimes been attributed to the non-progressive sociocultural conditions of a society that was dominated by slaveowners. In a similar vein, the low level of human capital in the Northeast has been explained in terms of the prevalence of slavery, and to the social and political conditions which militated against investment in the education of slaves. These interpretations of the Northeast's poorer economic experience are not convincing, however. As noted above, slavery was also common in the Southeast. Rather, the disparity in regional rates of economic development seems to have derived from major differences in the rates of growth of the two regions' exports during the nineteenth century.

We have seen elsewhere[14] that the overall pace of export expansion in nineteenth-century Brazil was relatively low. However, that aggregate picture obscures important differences in the pace of export growth by commodity and by region. In particular, overseas sales of coffee (which was produced mainly in the Southeast) increased much more rapidly than did exports of sugar and cotton (which were produced mainly in the Northeast). The difference in the export performance of the commodities in which the two regions specialized was large enough to transform the composition of Brazil's international trade. And quite apart from possible contrasts in linkage effects as between commodities, the disparity in rates of export growth was itself sufficiently large to generate significant differences in the pace of regional development.[15]

Table 2.1 presents information on the sharp drop in the share of sugar and cotton in total Brazilian export receipts during the nineteenth century. As the data indicate, at the beginning of the period, sugar and cotton, which were produced mainly in the Northeast, had accounted for nearly half of Brazil's export receipts. By 1912–14, however, the combined contribution of cotton and sugar had fallen to some 3 percent.[16] By contrast, coffee increased its share in total exports, and grew to dominate Brazil's foreign trade.

Table 2.1   *Share of Cotton, Sugar, and Coffee in Total Brazilian Export Receipts* (in percent)

Product	1821–23		1871–73		1912–14	
Cotton	25.8 ⎫		16.6 ⎫		2.9 ⎫	
Sugar	23.1 ⎭	48.9%	12.3 ⎭	28.9%	0.3 ⎭	3.2%
Coffee	18.7		50.2		60.4	

Source: Computed from data which are presented in Instituto Brasileiro de Geografia e Estatística, *Anuário Estatístico, 1939/1940* (Rio de Janeiro, 1941), pp. 1374–8.

This change in the composition of exports reflected the marked differences in the rate of growth of exports in these commodities during the nineteenth century. Table 2.2 presents data on the trend rates of growth of the income terms of trade, V_x/p_m, for Brazilian cotton, sugar, and coffee exports between 1822 and 1913. To permit some degree of disaggregation over this long time span, trend equations were also estimated for these series in two sub-periods, divided at the world depression year of 1873. As the data of Table 2.2 indicate, income from coffee exports grew at an annual trend rate appreciably higher than from cotton and sugar during the earlier period. After 1874, the disparity in export growth was even more marked. Coffee continued to expand, while cotton showed no trend. Overseas sales of sugar, however, experienced an absolute decline, at a precipitous rate.[17]

Export growth was of special importance for nineteenth-century Brazil, since the country's major export commodities were produced under conditions which made for a high foreign-trade multiplier.[18] Consequently, trends in export receipts were amplified in their impact on regional income. Further, export growth often led to investment in infrastructure facilities. The latter, in turn, provided external

Table 2.2   *Annual Trend Rate of Growth in the Income Terms of Trade of Brazilian Cotton, Sugar, and Coffee, 1822–1913* (in percent)

Product	1822–1913	1822–73	1874–1913
Cotton	1.4	4.1	*
Sugar	*	2.3	−7.0
Coffee	5.0	6.2	3.6

Notes: The asterisk indicates that the *t*-value of the trend term is not significant at the .05 level. The P_m index used in computing the income terms of trade series is the export price index (1880 prices) of Great Britain, Brazil's principal foreign supplier. This index is from Albert H. Imlah, *Economic Elements in the Pax Britannica* (Cambridge, Mass.: Harvard University Press, 1958), pp. 94–8. International transportation costs fell during the nineteenth century, so that Brazilian import prices could improve by a margin greater than indicated by the movement of British export prices. The fall in international transport costs, however, affected import costs of both the Northeast and of the Southeast by approximately the same extent. Consequently, the main point of Table 2.2 – a large disparity in the rates at which income from these exports grew – is still valid.

economies which facilitated development in other sectors of the regional economy. The Northeast was especially backward here, both in absolute and in relative terms. Thus in 1900, the entire region had only 1200 kilometers of public railway track, approximately 18 percent of the total for Brazil as a whole.[19]

The disparate pace of export growth was in fact associated with significant differences in the pace of industrial development and urbanization in the two regions. With the growth of regional income and a domestic market based on coffee exports, Brazil's expanding industrial sector was also concentrated in the provinces of Rio de Janeiro and São Paulo. The country's first cotton textile mills had been located mainly in the Northeast, a location which may have stemmed from the advantage of proximity to the Northeast's supplies of raw cotton. But despite that early advantage (and despite the external economies originating from initial production), Brazil's cotton textile industry gradually shifted to the Southeast. The Northeast's share in the industry fell from six of the country's nine cotton mills in 1866 to fourteen out of thirty in 1875; and to fifteen out of forty-eight in 1885.[20]

In reflection of greater growth in secondary and tertiary activities, urbanization proceeded at a more rapid pace in the Southeast. In the census of 1872, the combined population of the cities of Rio de Janeiro and São Paulo was already 50 percent greater than that of Bahia and Recife, the two major Northeastern cities. Taken in relation to the two regions' populations at that time, these figures indicate a higher rate of urbanization in the Southeast. In addition, between 1872 and 1900, the population of Rio de Janeiro increased at an annual rate of 3.7 percent, while São Paulo grew at an annual rate of 8.3 percent. By contrast, the population of Bahia increased at a rate of approximately 2.2 percent per annum, while that of Recife grew more slowly. These differential rates of urban growth led to an even greater difference in the extent of urbanization by region.[21]

Economic development in Brazil's Southeast occurred at a time when per capita income for the country as a whole was probably growing at a very low rate before 1900. At the beginning of the nineteenth century, the Southeast had more than one-third of Brazil's total population, while the Northeast had approximately one-half. Per capita income for the country as a whole is of course a weighted average for the country's various regions. Hence, positive income growth in the Southeast with its substantial weight implies that per capita income levels in the Northeast stagnated or even declined. The fragmentary data available do suggest a fall in the real wages of unskilled rural workers – the mass of the Northeast's population – in the last four decades of the century.[22] Whether the Northeast underwent an absolute as well as a relative decline in per capita income during the nineteenth century is not certain. What is clear, however, is that as a consequence of its economic experience during the nineteenth century, the Northeast began the twentieth century at a very low absolute level of underdevelopment and poverty.[23]

Some Questions

The preceding discussion raises some obvious questions. Why did Brazilian exports of sugar and cotton fare so badly as compared with coffee during the nineteenth century? Further, might not the Northeast's relatively poor export performance have been only a surface symptom which reflected profound differences in social or psychocultural aptitudes for economic development as between the Northeast and the Southeast?

The relatively slow growth of Brazil's sugar and cotton exports appears especially surprising, because these were two products for which world demand expanded rapidly during the nineteenth century. Cotton was, after all, one of the principal raw materials utilized in the industrial revolution of the period. Indeed, even after the first impact of the new technology had made itself felt in lower relative prices, the demand for cotton continued to expand vigorously. Between 1836–40 and 1876–1900, world trade in raw cotton increased almost eightfold, at annual rate of 3.5 percent.[24] Similarly, world consumption of sugar also grew enormously during the nineteenth century. Both rising income and the relatively high income elasticity of demand at prevailing income levels combined to produce this effect. Between 1841–45 and 1906–10, world sugar consumption rose no less than twelvefold.[25]

Cotton and sugar had long been produced in Brazil, and the country had ample resources to expand production both for the domestic and for the export markets.[26] In sugar and in cotton alike, however, Brazil had only a small share in major world markets. Further, the country's international market share in both products fell to still lower levels during the nineteenth century. Thus, Brazil supplied some 20 percent of Britain's raw cotton imports between 1801 and 1810; but the country's market share fell to 13 percent in the 1820s, and 3 percent in the 1840s. Responding to the special market conditions created by the American Civil War and the ensuing world cotton famine, Brazilian exports rose to 10 percent of British supply in the 1860s. By the 1870s, however, the figure was down to 6 percent; and in the 1880s, Brazil supplied less than 1 percent of the world market.[27] The country's position in the broader world market for cotton, including European demand, was still weaker. Brazil had a smaller share of this larger market, and its market share followed a similar downward trend in the course of the nineteenth century.[28]

The situation in sugar was similar. Brazilian exports had supplied some 10 percent of world sugar consumption in the 1840s. However, the country's portion of the international market declined persistently thereafter. Brazil's market share was 8 percent in the 1850s; 4 percent in the 1880s, and 2 percent in the 1890s. By the first decade of the twentieth century, Brazilian exports comprised less than 1 percent of the world market.[29]

In view of the rapid growth of world demand for cotton and sugar during the nineteenth century, Brazil's failure to expand its exports of these products much more vigorously seems astonishing. Numerous explanations have been proposed to explain this phenomenon. Although many of these interpretations are at least partly relevant, for the reasons discussed below, they are not completely convincing. Nevertheless, these explanations must be considered in some detail. First, they deal with substantive and analytical issues which are central for understanding the Northeast's failure to achieve significant economic development during the nineteenth century. Also, if we are not to repeat the same errors, it is essential to see why these earlier explanations are inadequate.

Some Earlier Explanations, Market Conditions

One explanation of the slow growth of Brazil's cotton and sugar exports has stressed (non-market) limitations on the demand side. In particular, Roberto Simonsen suggested that Brazilian exports to some major world markets were hampered because of the colonial preferences imposed by the British, French, and Dutch in favor of imports from their own empires.[30] For example, an 1810 treaty between Brazil and the United Kingdom excluded Brazilian sugar, tobacco, and coffee from the British market during the first half of the century.

Colonial policies undoubtedly did influence the geographical distribution of Brazilian exports during the nineteenth century. Nevertheless, this interpretation leaves important questions unanswered. Why did Brazilian exports of coffee to the American market (which was not restricted during most of the century) grow so much more rapidly than Brazilian exports of sugar to the United States? Similarly, why, despite colonial restrictions, did Brazilian coffee exports do so much better in the world market than did Brazilian exports of sugar and cotton? The poor performance of Brazil's cotton exports appears especially puzzling in the context of Simonsen's interpretation. Colonial preferences may help explain the fact that Brazil's cotton exports did even worse in some European markets than in Great Britain. Great Britain, however, was by far the largest market for raw cotton during the nineteenth century. And even before the advent of free trade (in mid-century), Brazilian cotton had not been impeded from entering the British market. The interpretation in terms of colonial preferences is especially inadequate here because the largest supplier of cotton to the British market was the United States, not a British colony. Brazil's failure to participate more effectively in the expanding international market for cotton therefore requires further data and discussion.

Brazil's initial cotton exports were largely of a tree-grown variety which yielded a long-staple fiber. Between 1811 and 1855, this variety commanded a price premium of 25–35 percent over the short-staple cotton produced in the United States.[31] Consequently, one might suppose that Brazil's small and declining share of the world cotton trade reflected nothing more than a concentration on the premium segment of the market, which happened to be growing relatively slowly. Such an interpretation is belied, however, by the data of Table 2.3. This table presents information on the quantum of Brazil's cotton exports. The Brazilian figures are shown alongside the export statistics for Egypt and Smyrna, producers who also specialized in long-staple cotton. As the data indicate, Brazil's cotton exports were small and relatively stagnant (with a declining market share) not only in relation to the United States, but also *vis-à-vis* other producers of long-staple cotton.

After 1850, new spinning techniques eroded much of the price differential which long-staple cotton had earlier commanded. Brazilian producers responded to the changed market conditions by shifting increasingly to short-staple varieties.[32] This switch to the

Table 2.3 *Raw Cotton Supply from Brazil and Other Suppliers in Imports to British, American and European Manufacturing, 1836–1900*

Period	Brazil	Egypt, Smyrna	United States	Other	Total	Brazil relative to total (%)
		(millions of lb, annual averages)				
1836–40	25	30	586	70	711	3.5
1841–45	19	24	816	82	941	2.0
1846–50	24	30	964	93	1111	2.2
1851–55	27	60	1255	141	1483	1.8
1856–60	28	57	1634	215	1934	1.5
1861–65	36	191	532	506	1265	2.9
1866–70	100	191	1109	610	2009	5.0
1871–75	109	238	1682	581	2610	4.2
1876–80	44	269	2232	423	2967	1.5
1881–85	54	293	2717	552	3616	1.5
1886–90	52	302	3170	597	4121	1.3
1891–95	51	456	3774	467	4747	1.1
1896–1900	25	576	4595	316	5511	0.5

Source: Adapted from data of the British Board of Trade which are presented in D. C. M. Platt, *Latin America and British Trade, 1806–1914* (New York: Harper & Row, 1973), p. 257.

broader segment of the market failed to induce a substantial long-term increase in Brazil's cotton exports. Thus, in response to the higher cotton prices of the 1860s, Brazil's exports and international market share rose (see Table 2.3). But by the 1870s, following reconstruction after the American Civil War, the United States returned to large-scale exportation. Thereupon, Brazil's cotton exports diminished sharply, and the country's share of the total market fell steadily, to reach levels below those of the 1860s. As this discussion indicates, the slow growth of cotton exports from nineteenth-century Brazil seems to have reflected an inability to compete effectively in the international economy; it cannot be attributed to a concentration on the long-staple market.

Brazil's poor performance in sugar exports has also been ascribed to special market conditions. For example, until mid-century, colonial preferences put Brazilian sugar at a disadvantage *vis-à-vis* the British West Indies in competition for the rapidly growing British market. In the late 1840s, however, these institutional barriers were removed. Despite this change, Brazil's sugar exports did not increase sharply. Even when competing without a colonial handicap, Brazilian exports were unable to gain a major share in the British market.[33]

Later in the nineteenth century, cane sugar such as was produced in Brazil suffered increasingly from the competition of European beet sugar.[34] By the 1860s, the major continental countries applied import restrictions to protect their local producers. And beginning in the 1870s, European producers 'dumped' large quantities of beet sugar in the British market. Similarly, in 1903 the United States accorded special tariff preferences to sugar produced in Cuba, Puerto Rico, and Hawaii. These conditions, however, fail to account for the slow growth of Brazil's sugar exports during the nineteenth century. Thus the growth of beet sugar production does not explain the sharp fall in Brazil's share of the international market in *cane* sugar.[35] And Brazil's percentage of total sugar production had been small (and declining) since the 1840s – long before the special trade distortions which the European governments imposed to protect beet sugar production. By the same token, the US tariff preferences introduced at the beginning of the twentieth century cannot be invoked to explain the poor performance of Brazilian sugar in the American market during the nineteenth century.

Finally, two other market-related explanations of Brazil's lagging exports must be considered. One concerns Brazil's competition with Cuba for the expanding sugar market in the United States. In principle, Brazil's relatively poor performance before the 1903 tariff preferences may simply have reflected Cuba's greater proximity and lower transport costs to the United States. That hypothesis, however, is not borne out empirically. The research of David Denslow indicates that higher wage costs in Cuba more than offset that country's transport-cost advantage *vis-à-vis* Brazil.[36]

Another interpretation has focused on the diversion (in the last decades of the century) of the Northeast's sugar and cotton production from the international market to internal demand within Brazil.[37] By the 1860s, a cotton textile industry had emerged in Brazil, which took an increasingly large share of the country's raw cotton output. Similarly, the Northeast sold increasing quantities of sugar within Brazil, to the markets of the Southeast. That market was protected by a tariff, and prices there were above world market levels.[38] Hence it may be suggested that declining overseas sales simply reflected a diversion of the Northeast's output to the more lucrative domestic market. This explanation is not helpful in the present context, however, for two reasons. Large-scale sales of cotton and sugar to the internal market began only in the last half of the nineteenth century. Hence, this interpretation does not explain the Northeast's poor export performance during much of the period under consideration. More generally, the proposed explanation might be plausible under conditions of fixed output and factor supplies. The Northeast, however, had ample resources for expanding cotton and sugar output.[39] Greater quantities of these commodities could have been produced to supply both domestic and international markets on a larger scale if the Northeast's costs had been competitive.[40]

Some Earlier Explanations, Cost Conditions

Other interpretations have attributed the poor performance of Brazil's sugar and cotton exports to unfavorable supply conditions. For example, a contemporary British observer stressed the importance of labor shortages which allegedly hampered Brazilian cotton production after the cessation, in 1852, of overseas slave importation.[41] Note, however, that the share of Brazilian cotton exports in the British market had also fallen during the earlier decades, when large-scale importation of slaves from Africa was feasible. And Brazil's market share continued to decline despite a fall in wages after the 1860s in the Northeast's major province of Pernambuco.[42]

Other writers have emphasized the constraint on cotton exports which was imposed by the high internal transportation costs of the pre-railroad era in Brazil.[43] Although transport costs were undoubtedly important in nineteenth-century Brazil, it is not clear that they can explain the pattern of export growth *by commodity*. Moreover, some railways were later built which directly or indirectly lowered freight charges from a number of the potential cotton-producing areas in the Northeast. This development did not lead to a long-term increase in the country's cotton exports. The failure of cotton exports to expand is especially noteworthy in this instance because when railway construction was completed, large numbers of workers were released, putting downward pressure on wages. Thus wages and transport costs tended to fall conjointly. Finally, and perhaps most disturbing for the transport-cost hypothesis, is something which did *not* happen. I refer to the fact that British (or other) capitalists did not build railways more deeply into the Northeast's cotton region. The paucity of railroad investment in Brazil's cotton zones is striking in view of British efforts to increase and diversify the cotton textile industry's raw material supplies during the nineteenth century. Clearly, foreign investors did not anticipate that the reduction in transport costs following railway construction in the Northeast would generate a large volume of cotton exports and freight revenue. This experience offers a notable contrast with coffee, where market prospects were favorable, and infrastructure facilities were provided on a much larger scale.

Supply rigidities on the part of individual producers might also explain the Northeast's failure to enlarge its sugar and cotton exports more vigorously in the face of a rapidly expanding world market. In principle, such supply constraints might stem from either (or both) of two sources: inflexibilities of social structure, or cultural norms which led to (economically) non-optimizing behavior due to tradition-bound attitudes in an allegedly pre-capitalist society. Although an interpretation along those lines may be appealing in *a priori* terms, it is inconsistent in the context of the historical information available about this society. First, Brazil's cotton producers did in fact demonstrate an ability to expand output rapidly when market conditions warranted. Thus, reacting to the opportunities of the world cotton famine, Brazilian cotton exports rose from an annual average of 28 million lb in 1856–60 to 100 million lb in 1866–70 (see Table 2.3). And by the same token, the subsequent contraction of cotton exports also indicates a freedom from rigidities in determining production patterns. In this instance, producers in the Northeast reduced cotton production rather than proceed autoregressively and accept unremunerative prices. Similarly, although the Northeast's sugar was produced in a planter-dominated society, this need not have precluded capitalistic behavior and responsiveness to economic incentives. As noted earlier, coffee in the Southeast was also produced in the context of the social relations and cultural norms of a slave-owning society. Moreover, some members of the Northeast sugar aristocracy who appear to fit the stereotype of seigneurs glorying in conspicuous consumption were also among those who plowed back profits and modernized their facilities.[44]

Furthermore, supply equations which have been estimated for Brazil's sugar and cotton in the nineteenth century indicate the presence of microeconomic rationality and price-responsive behavior in the Northeast.[45] And despite putative sociocultural constraints, planters in the Northeast seem to have obtained cane yields per hectare as high as those of Cuba, a relatively efficient producer.[46] Output per worker may have been lower in the Northeast. However, to explain Brazil's small and declining share in the international sugar market it does not suffice to note that productivity was lower in the Northeast than in other sugar-producing areas. The effects of the Northeast's lower productivity levels on exports could in principle have been offset by lower factor returns in the region. The research of David Denslow, who compared productivity levels and monetary costs in the Northeast with those of Cuba, indicates that this offsetting condition was met in Brazil until the last two decades of the nineteenth century.[47] Further, accounts which attempt to explain Brazil's declining share in the world market in terms of the Northeast's low productivity are also inadequate for another, more general reason. Those interpretations fail to explain why Brazil's exchange rate did not adjust to permit large exports despite low productivity levels.

Another version of the productivity argument, cast in dynamic terms, has also received currency. Thus it has been suggested that although the Northeast producers may have demonstrated micro-economic rationality and an absence of supply rigidities with given production functions, they lagged in introducing new and more productive techniques. Brazilian cotton producers were in fact technologically backward as compared with producers in other countries.[48] Similarly in sugar, the Northeast lagged two and three decades behind Louisiana and Cuba in the introduction of technical innovations in the milling process and in the conversion from water to steam power.[49] This behavior cannot always be attributed to the existence of different relative factor prices in Brazil, for some of the innovations seem to have saved capital and materials as well as labor. Sociocultural constraints and/or capital-market imperfections have been proposed as the underlying reasons for the lags in adopting more productive, modern technology.[50]

This interpretation which emphasizes technological backwardness as the cause of the Northeast's poor export performance may be attractive in *a priori* terms. However, the explanation is insufficient in this historical context. As noted above, exchange-rate movements and (until the end of the century) lower factor returns could have offset the impact of technological lags on export growth. Further, the interpretation of the Northeast's poor export achievement in terms of the failure to introduce modern technology is not consistent with the results of a unique historical experiment which began in the 1870s.[51] The Brazilian government accepted a version of the technological backwardness interpretation that we have been discussing, and attempted to help the Northeast by promoting technological modernization of the sugar industry. The government proceeded by offering foreign firms special concessions to introduce modern, large-scale sugar mills. The government also reduced uncertainty and risk for the foreigners by guaranteeing minimum returns. Nevertheless, there were difficulties in finding foreign investors to take up the concessions. This reluctance turned out to be well-justified. Many of the enterprises which were finally launched using more modern technology made losses rather than profits.

Numerous hypotheses have been advanced to explain this failure. For example, some accounts have suggested poor management and/or bad faith on the part of the foreign concessionaires. Other interpretations have cited unwillingness of the Northeast's planters to supply the new mills with cane (at the terms offered). Far from constituting an explanation, however, the persistence of these problems beyond the initial period when the new mills were first installed only sharpens the puzzle. For if the new technology had really permitted high profits (as the technological backwardness interpretation implies), it would have paid the concessionaires to invest and make the arrangements necessary to overcome such difficulties. Their failure to do so suggests that some conditions were present in the Northeast which made the use of the new technology less profitable than in other sugar-producing regions.

Some of the new mills were subsequently sold (at depreciated capital values) to Brazilian owners; and the new mills continued to operate. The problem of cane supply was resolved through vertical integration; that is, the processing firms invested in agricultural production, and supplied much of the cane which their mills required. Brazilian governments also subsidized another wave of investment in mills that used modern, larger-scale production techniques (*usinas*). Notwithstanding their more advanced technology, however, many of the *usinas* apparently also failed to earn positive returns.[52]

Even more strikingly, introduction of the new technology obviously did not stem the dramatic decline of Brazil's overseas sugar exports. Between 1883 and 1913, their sterling value fell at an annual trend rate of 9.6 percent. Those years were part of a troubled period in the world sugar market. Supply increases intensified and falling prices were common. But what is pertinent here is the fact that Brazil's receipts from sugar declined much more precipitously than did those of all other exporting countries. For example, Mauritius, one of the more seriously affected sugar producers, saw the value of its export revenue fall at an annual rate of some 2 percent.[53] As indicated, this decline was much less than in Brazil. In the West Indies, the dollar value of exports remained virtually constant. And to heighten the contrast, the value of Cuban exports rose at a rate of almost 2 percent per annum during this period. Thus not only did technological modernization fail to improve the Northeast's export performance, but special factors seem to have amplified the impact which adverse international market conditions had on the region's exports.

We will consider one further explanation. David Denslow has proposed an interpretation of Brazil's poor experience in sugar exports during the last part of the period, toward the end of the nineteenth century.[54] His analysis focuses on technology and costs in the Northeast and Cuba. Technological developments in the last years of the century, he suggests, greatly increased the optimal scale of production in sugar extraction and refining. In order to take full advantage of these scale economies, sugar factories had to utilize larger amounts of cane, transported from much greater distances. Because of the Northeast's soil patterns and hilly terrain, however, transport costs were high. Consequently, Brazilian producers were unable to exploit the new large-scale technology to its maximum efficiency. As a result, their production costs fell less than did those of Cuban producers, whose topography was well-suited to the new technology.

Despite its appeal, this interpretation encounters some problems in the present context. The analysis does not explain (nor is it intended to explain) Brazil's small and declining share of the world sugar market over most of the century. The time interval we are considering extends from 1822 to 1913. But it was only toward the end of that period that the new refining technology was embodied in a large fraction of the capital stock of Brazil's competitors in the international sugar market. More generally, Denslow's analysis is not appropriate for the problem at hand – explaining why Brazil's sugar and cotton exports grew so much more slowly than the country's overseas sales of coffee. This is because a country's exports are determined by comparative rather than by absolute advantage. And 'comparative' refers here to the relative costs of different commodities within an individual country rather than the cost of the same commodity in different countries. Consequently, the relevant comparison for the present purpose is not in terms of factor productivity or monetary costs in sugar as between Brazil and Cuba. In order to explain the export performance of different products within Brazil, we must focus on productivity and returns in Brazilian sugar as compared with productivity and returns in Brazil's other exportable products such as coffee.[55]

The same analytical limitation also reduces the usefulness of the other cost-oriented interpretations which we discussed above. Those hypotheses, too, attempt to explain Brazil's poor export performance in sugar and cotton by referring to conditions which made for high costs in Brazil as compared with other producing countries. Such analyses may be illuminating in suggesting why Brazil had high factor or monetary costs in specific commodities. But because comparative advantage is what matters in this context, those interpretations are insufficient to explain the disparity in rates of export growth by commodity within Brazil.[56]

An Explanation of the Disparity in Rates of Export Growth

For the reasons discussed, the earlier explanations proposed are insufficient. However, upon reflection, a straightforward answer to our question suggests itself. Exports of coffee increased more rapidly than did exports of sugar and cotton because Brazilian comparative advantage favored coffee, and higher returns could be obtained in that activity than in sugar or cotton. This interpretation would indeed be too obvious to be worth discussing were it not for the misperceptions introduced by the earlier explanations. Also, in the historical conditions that prevailed in Brazil during the nineteenth century, comparative advantage operated through some mechanisms which are of special analytical and policy interest.

We have available an unambiguous test for verifying this interpretation. Brazil did not abolish slavery until 1888. Consequently, the data on the allocation of the country's slave-labor force can be used as a source of information not only about regional levels of per capita income, but also concerning Brazilian comparative advantage in the products in which the different regions specialized. This is because the deployment of the country's stock of slaves provides an indication of the relative marginal value product of labor and of the relative rates of return to the capital (invested in slaves) which were employed in the country's various economic activities. Such information on relative factor returns, in turn, is a clear indicator of comparative advantage in diverse commodities.

During most of the century, the returns available in cotton were apparently below those that could be obtained in other export activities. This is indicated by the fact that cotton was generally not produced in a plantation system, using slaves, but was planted on a small scale by individuals too poor to have access to the capital needed for sugar and other plantation crops.[57] Also, in a shift in which a movement of relative prices appears to have played a part, rates of return and the marginal value-product of labor seem to have moved in favor of coffee and against sugar.[58] Evidence for this change is provided by the fact that during the century the Southeastern coffee planters were able to bid a substantial part of the slave-labor force away from the Northeast.[59] Table 2.4 presents data on this shift. As noted earlier, by the time slavery was abolished, approximately 75 percent of the slave population was located in the coffee region of Rio de Janeiro, São Paulo and Minas Gerais.

This movement of factors into the activities with higher returns was incomplete, however. As late as 1872, some 47 percent of Brazil's

Table 2.4   *Regional Distribution of Brazil's Population, 1823 and 1872* (in percent)

Region	Slave Population		Free Population		Total Population	
	1823	1872	1823	1872	1823	1872
North	3	2	3	4	3	3
Northeast	54	32	51	49	52	47
Southeast	39	59	37	37	38	40
South	1	6	7	7	5	7
Central West	3	1	2	2	2	2

Note: See n. 1, above, for the definition of the various regions.

Source: Computed from data cited in Stanley J. Stein, *Vassouras: A Brazilian Coffee County, 1850–1900* (Cambridge, Mass.: Harvard University Press, 1957), p. 296.

population was still in the Northeast (see Table 2.4). There is no need to posit economic irrationality to account for this continuing disparity in factor productivity, for there were important costs and constraints on resource reallocation.

The heavy transportation costs between the regions of Brazil, of course, reduced the flow of labor for any given wage differential.[60] And the relatively high capital costs which prevailed in nineteenth-century Brazil also lowered the amount of investment in migration. In addition, the reallocation of slaves to the Southeast was restricted by the taxes that were imposed for a time in an effort to stop the movement.[61] Further insight into why the movement of labor was so limited is provided by the fact that, despite these barriers, the inter-regional migration was much greater for slaves than for the free population (see Table 2.4).

First, free labor was not used widely in the major export activities of the Southeast until the 1880s, so that the demand for free workers was limited. In addition, transportation costs were lower for slaves than for free migrants.[62] Further, on the supply side, the slave-labor market provided a mechanism for financing the capital costs of interregional labor reallocation of slaves. No comparable capital-market facilities were available to finance migration by the free population. Finally, most of the special types of land (and climate) of the Northeast were not well-suited for coffee production, and had higher returns in other activities. Hence, in cases of landowners whose income was derived from a combination of land, capital, and entrepreneurship inputs, reallocation of factors to coffee was also impeded. Because of these conditions which affected the costs of factor reallocation, although part of Brazil's slave-labor force was transferred to the Southeast, the overall factor movement was not large.

Land and Imperfect Factor Reallocation

The preceding discussion emphasized the importance of the limited reallocation of productive factors from sugar and cotton to coffee. Implicit in that discussion were some conditions associated with Brazil's endowment of land. This is a factor which is sometimes neglected; but because of its importance in an agrarian economy like nineteenth-century Brazil, some key points should be noted.

Land was not a uniform or homogeneous factor, in the sense of having identical technical properties and hence equal returns in all activities. On the contrary, the special types of land (and climate) in the Northeast had higher returns in activities other than coffee. Land was thus not a mobile factor; consequently, inter*sectoral* reallocation of other factors required *geographical* mobility. Furthermore, because of Brazil's endowment of land and high-cost transportation facilities, the costs of this reallocation were relatively high. With the country's abundant land, cultivation was extensive and population densities were low. Hence, the distances from the interior to the borders of Brazil's various regions were large. Transfer costs were also high because of the great distances between the country's distinct regions. Both on interregional and on intraregional grounds, then, the geographical movements that were required for factor reallocation in this vast country were large.

The availability of low-cost transportation facilities such as railways would have helped this situation by reducing costs and permitting labor to escape from the Northeast and its low returns. But as discussed elsewhere,[63] Brazil did not experience large-scale railroad construction until late in the nineteenth century. And when railroad construction did accelerate, factor reallocation to the Southeast was limited by other conditions. Beginning in the 1880s, with the impending demise of slavery, the government subsidized large-scale immigration from Europe. Most of the European immigrants went to satisfy the growing labor demands of the Southeast. However, similar subsidies were not provided to lower the private costs of internal migration from the Northeast to the Southeast. Under these conditions, the Southeast coffee planters found it cheaper to import labor from Italy than from the Northeast. This circumstance, too, reduced the magnitude of internal factor reallocation.[64]

What happened to the Northeast during the nineteenth century, then, was a shift in Brazilian comparative advantage away from the products in which the region specialized. Changes in comparative advantage which are location-specific occur in many economies.[65] The adjustment process was more difficult in Brazil, however, because of the special conditions which impeded factor reallocation. Consequently, there was a major difference between Brazil's historical experience and simple textbook models of comparative advantage. The beneficial welfare effects of those models require that resources be reallocated with little delay and cost to the activity toward which comparative advantage has shifted. In the case of the Northeast, however, the factors of production which had previously been employed in sugar and cotton generally did not move geographically to be employed, at higher returns, in coffee.

The plight of the Northeast was also aggravated by the fact that international prices of its export staples were greatly affected by the supply of countries (e.g. Cuba and the West Indies) whose internal comparative-advantage conditions were very different from those of Brazil. In those producing areas, local conditions led to higher returns in sugar than in other potential export commodities. Consequently, those areas increased their output (and may thus have depressed prices still further) in response to prices which Brazilian producers found unremunerative. Finally, the situation of the Northeast was exacerbated by certain effects which stemmed from the operation of Brazil's exchange-rate system. This accentuated the negative impact of the shift in comparative advantage, and gave a second-stage impulse to the process which was to make the Northeast a backward region within Brazil.

The Exchange-Rate Mechanism Under Imperfect Factor Reallocation

The shift in comparative advantage also affected Brazil's international exchange rate. The fact that the country's comparative advantage lay in coffee meant that foreign exchange could be earned at a lower *mil-réis* cost in coffee than in sugar or cotton. That is, the domestic resource cost of a unit of foreign exchange was smaller in coffee than in the export commodities produced in the Northeast.[66] Consequently, Brazilian coffee could be exported at world market prices with an exchange rate that gave fewer *mil-réis* per pound sterling. By contrast, many producers of sugar and cotton in Brazil could compete on world markets only with a *mil-réis*/sterling parity that was relatively high. Stated in other terms: the country's unitary exchange rate implied a *mil-réis* which was undervalued from the viewpoint of coffee, but overvalued from the viewpoint of sugar and cotton. This situation initiated a self-reinforcing dynamic which hurt the Northeast in powerful ways.

The *mil-réis* price which exporters of each commodity received in Brazil was determined by two factors: the particular commodity's world market (sterling) price, and the country's overall exchange rate. Movements in Brazil's external parity during the nineteenth century were determined by many conditions, including the country's rate of monetary expansion and the level of world coffee prices.[67] At any point in time, however, coffee exports led to a stronger *mil-réis* than would have been the case in the absence of coffee exports. This occurred not only because of the additional supply of foreign exchange which coffee generated, but also because the domestic resource cost of foreign exchange was relatively low in Brazil's coffee sector.[68] Consequently, as coffee exports grew to dominate Brazil's foreign trade, the exchange rate increasingly reflected the weight of coffee and its pressures for a lower *mil-réis*/sterling exchange rate than would otherwise have prevailed.

Such pressures on Brazil's external parity had a major impact on the local-currency prices received by the country's sugar and cotton producers (see below). *Mil-réis* prices, in turn, affected both the magnitude of factor earnings and the level of output in those activities. As noted earlier, the supply of sugar and of cotton in nineteenth-century Brazil varied positively in function of the *mil-réis* prices offered. The height of the *mil-réis* price for each commodity was thus crucial, for it helped determine both the volume of exports and the value (price multiplied by volume) of factor incomes in those activities.

Our discussion of the exchange-rate mechanism's effects has emphasized the role of Brazil's unitary parity in determining the *mil-réis* prices of the Northeast's exports. In order to ascertain the relative importance of changes in the overall exchange rate and of each commodity's sterling price in accounting for movements of the *mil-réis* price for sugar and cotton, the following procedure was adopted. The annual *mil-réis* price of each commodity is equal to the sum of the logarithm of the product's sterling price and the logarithm of the country's *mil-réis*/sterling exchange rate. Hence, the variance of the logarithm of the annual observations of each commodity's *mil-réis* price can be analyzed in terms of the variances (and the covariance) of the logarithms of these two terms. Table 2.5 presents the results of this decomposition for two periods, 1822–73 and 1874–1913.[69]

Table 2.5 shows that even in the earlier period, variations in the exchange rate had been more important than variations in sugar's sterling price in accounting for changes in the *mil-réis* price of Brazil's

Table 2.5 *Relative Contribution of the Variance of the Brazilian Exchange Rate of Each Commodity's Sterling Price, and of the Covariance Term to the Total Variance of the* Mil-Réis *Price of Brazil's Sugar and Cotton Exports* (in percent)

Product and Period	Var In ER	Var In£p_i	Cov (ER, £p_i)
Sugar, 1822–73	115	91	−53
1874–1913	83	31	−7
Cotton, 1822–73	32	79	−5
1874–1913	69	20	6

Note: These percentages were computed from the following formula: Var In *mil-réis* p_i=Var (In *ER*)+Var (In£p_i)+2 Cov (In *ER*, In£p_i), where *ER* denotes the *mil-réis* sterling exchange rate, and £p_i denotes each commodity's sterling price.

sugar exports.[70] After the 1870s, however, exchange-rate variations became by far the major determinant of variations in the local-currency price of sugar. The situation in cotton was similar. In that commodity, too, movements in the exchange rate became much more quantitatively important than changes in the sterling price in determining the change of the *mil-réis* price.

Thus the following process seems to have operated. For the reasons discussed earlier, factor reallocation from the Northeast to the Southeast (and from sugar and cotton to coffee) was limited. Both regions, however, had to face the same external parity – the lower *mil-réis*/sterling rate which reflected coffee's dominance in the country's foreign-exchange market.[71] Under these conditions, the exchange-rate mechanism greatly accentuated the impact of declining comparative advantage on the economy of the Northeast. The lower *mil-réis*/sterling parity meant that producers in the region received fewer *mil-réis* for their sugar and cotton exports. Lower local-currency prices, of course, meant lower income for the factors of production which were engaged in the Northeast's sugar and cotton production. And unfortunately, few alternative opportunities which offered better conditions were available in the region. Consequently, factor incomes in the Northeast were pushed toward the levels offered in the best alternative occupation, the region's low-productivity subsistence agriculture.

The exchange-rate mechanism also slowed the pace of technical progress in the Northeast's sugar and cotton production. Lower *mil-réis* prices led to smaller profits which could be used to finance investment in improved techniques. Further, the lower local-currency prices which resulted from the exchange-rate mechanism may have been the underlying cause of the situation noted earlier, in which technological innovations that were profitable in other countries yielded returns too low to justify adoption in Brazil. Under these conditions, the delays and failures of technological modernization in the Northeast during the nineteenth century are not surprising.

The exchange-rate mechanism also reduced the quantity of sugar and cotton exports in another, more direct manner. With given world prices but a higher *mil-réis*/sterling parity, the volume of the Northeast's exports would have been larger despite the numerous cost and market problems which we discussed earlier. But with upward-sloping supply curves for sugar and cotton (due to differential soil fertility and transport costs), the existence of lower prices in domestic currency meant a smaller quantity of exports from the region in any year. Moreover, the negative effects on output, income, and employment in the Northeast's advanced sector grew progressively worse during the century. As coffee enlarged its share in Brazil's total supply of foreign exchange, the pressure on the country's exchange rate increased. Hence, the degree of exchange-rate overvaluation for sugar and cotton grew over time, in a self-sustaining process. In the course of the nineteenth century, this process priced ever-greater quantities of the Northeast's sugar and cotton out of world markets.[72]

Finally, the unitary exchange-rate mechanism also crippled the region's adjustment to the post-1880 fall in world sugar prices. Other producing countries could respond to declining prices with exchange-rate depreciation and quantity increases. Thus in cases where producers lacked an economic alternative that was superior to sugar, they could maintain (or, as we have noted, even increase) the foreign exchange value of their exports. Such a parity adjustment was precluded for the Northeast, however, because the foreign exchange supplied by coffee was also present in the country's unified exchange market. Thus the exchange-rate mechanism effectively constrained the regional adjustment process. Further, this mechanism aggravated the impact on the Northeast of falling international sugar prices. These conditions help explain why Brazil's sugar exports declined so much more rapidly than those of other sugar producers after the 1880s.

The various effects of the exchange-rate mechanism were mutually reinforcing in their consequences for the economy of the Northeast. Thus economic growth in the region suffered because both the quantities *and* the prices of exports were adversely affected. And factor returns were held down not only by low product prices, but also by the meager increase in physical productivity. Further, the unfavorable economic conditions for technological progress frustrated individual or governmental efforts to reverse the shift in comparative advantage and thereby expand overseas sales of sugar and cotton. Finally, stagnant technology compounded the effects of increasing exchange overvaluation on growth of the Northeast's exports.

The economic plight of the Northeast during the nineteenth century originated, then, in the fact that Brazil's comparative advantage had shifted from sugar and cotton to coffee. The price and quantity signals which brought this message home to producers were amplified, however, by the exchange-rate effects we have discussed. Unfortunately, these amplified signals were of little help in indicating a solution to the problem. And the consequences of the price and quantity changes were especially brutal because of the circumstances which constrained interregional factor reallocation. Under those conditions, the market's signals did not stimulate an equilibrating adjustment process. Further, an effective public policy response was also not feasible (see below). What the Northeast needed was a *mil- réis*/sterling parity which was consistently higher than the Southeast's external parity. But the technique of multiple exchange rates had not yet been invented, and thus was not part of the social technology available in the nineteenth century.[73]

Neither the market mechanism nor government action, then, could do much to save the Northeast from its unhappy economic experience. And all a later observer can do is to recognize that the process we have noted helps make comprehensible an otherwise puzzling situation: the poor growth experience of the Northeast's exports in the midst of a rapidly expanding international (and national) economy.

Currency-Union Effects and Regional Divergence

The Northeast's links with the national economy may indeed have made things worse. For historical and political reasons, the Northeast was part of the same political unit as the rest of Brazil. But as we have seen, the Northeast and the Southeast did not satisfy a basic condition required for a well-functioning currency union – interregional labor mobility.[74] The ensuing currency-union effects appear to have further aggravated economic conditions in the Northeast.

As part of the same political unit, the Northeast was obliged to maintain a fixed, one-to-one *mil-réis* 'exchange rate' in its transactions with the Southeast. Taken together with the Northeast's exchange overvaluation *vis-à-vis* the rest of the world, this parity within Brazil implies that the region's exchange rate in relation to the Southeast may also have been overvalued. Thus to the extent that the economies of the two regions were (or could have been) complementary, regional overvaluation reduced the magnitude of the Northeast's exports to the growing Southeast, as compared with what they would have been under a different exchange regime. Some exports, particularly of sugar and cotton, did proceed from the Northeast to the coffee region. Under conditions of exchange overvaluation, however, such trade would have involved interregional payments disequilibrium for the Northeast. Resolution of such a disequilibrium required economic shifts which hampered the Northeast's development.

The stock of nationally marketable financial assets which could be transferred from the Northeast to finance an interregional trade deficit was limited mainly to money. There are in fact indications of a chronic scarcity of liquidity and of higher interest rates in the Northeast.[75] Such conditions must have lowered capital formation and activity levels in the region. These illiquidity pressures were compounded by another feature of the currency union – the requirement that the Northeast's exchange rate *vis-à-vis* the rest of Brazil remain fixed. Parity changes were thus precluded as a mechanism for adjusting interregional over-valuation.[76] Hence, the pressures for equilibrium involved a deflationary bias for the Northeast and, with wages rigid downwards at the subsistence level, lower levels of real output and employment. Again, this is consistent with the reports from the region.[77] These deflationary effects of currency union were especially serious for the

Northeast, for they affected the domestic sector as well as the region's export activities.

The currency-union effects, exchange-rate conditions, and factor reallocation costs we have discussed were all part of the Northeast's macroeconomic environment during the nineteenth century. Consequently, mechanisms to reverse the Northeast's decline and induce a convergence of regional development were notable for their absence in nineteenth-century Brazil.[78] Indeed because of the exchange-rate mechanism, the growth of coffee exports from the Southeast led directly to an accelerating decline in overseas sales of the Northeast's sugar and cotton. At the same time, growing exchange overvaluation reduced the interregional linkage effects which were presumably the Northeast's chief economic benefit from being in the same political unit as the Southeast. Finally, there was no tendency toward decreasing returns to scale in the Southeast's economic activities. On the contrary, external economies and infrastructure facilities such as railways which resulted from the Southeast's growth in earlier periods facilitated subsequent development in that region, both in manufacturing and in agriculture. For example, when internal relative prices shifted to favor cotton and sugar in the twentieth century, the Southeast outdid the Northeast in increasing the production of these commodities, both for exports and for the domestic market.

The political system also failed to cushion the Northeast from the regional economic shift. By the 1830s the Northeast no longer exerted undue influence on Brazilian national politics. In the aggregate, government allocation policies displayed no tendency to favor the Northeast.[79] In the 1870s and 1880s, the central government did extend some help to the region after periods of catastrophic drought. But like the program for introducing modern sugar technology, this aid was not very effective in inducing regional convergence. More generally, the Northeast's economic weakness did not provide the basis for a strong political position within Brazilian national politics. Consequently, the region was not able to use the country's political system in order to promote economic resurgence. It was only in the middle of the twentieth century that more effectual government programs were implemented to help the Northeast.[80]

The Northeast as a Separate Political Unit?

Under these conditions, one may wonder whether the Northeast would not have been better off economically as a separate political unit, with its own currency system and exchange rate. The Northeast's trade and development would then have been governed by its own (rather than by Brazilian) comparative advantage. Such liberation would have spared the region the pernicious effects of the exchange-rate mechanism on the level and growth of its overseas exports. In addition, the Northeast would have avoided the debilitating consequences of the currency union on its domestic sector.

As part of Brazil, the Northeast did have one advantage. The Southeast offered the Northeast a market for domestic sugar sales, and at prices that were above world-market levels. During most of the nineteenth century, however, the quantitative importance of these domestic sales was small.[81] And the total volume of exports – a relevant consideration in a region with underutilized land and labor – was much smaller than it would have been if the Northeast had enjoyed undistorted access to the entire world market. Further, the welfare gains from interregional exports were reduced because of another condition. In the second half of the century, Brazil maintained significant import tariffs.[82] These raised the prices of many commodities imported from overseas or from the Southeast above world-market levels; accordingly, the value, in international prices, of the Northeast's interregional exports to the Southeast was reduced. Finally, interregional exports failed to compensate for lower overseas sales in another respect. The decline in the Northeast's overseas exports reduced the region's access to foreign capital, private and public. It was such foreign-capital inflow that helped provide the Southeast with its more ample infrastructure facilities. And the latter were more important both for domestic agricultural development and for industrial growth in the Southeast.[83]

Obviously, the advantages and disadvantages of political independence for the Northeast cannot be discussed with reference to economics alone. The maintenance of the country's territorial integrity was a value which many Brazilians have cherished deeply, both in the nineteenth century and thereafter. However, the net economic loss which political unity entailed may be considered as the 'price' that was paid for such meta-economic values. Further, an assessment of the price (or tradeoffs) which were present in nineteenth-century Brazil's regional divergence is of particular interest because this case involved a special feature. The tradeoff here was not between higher economic growth and increased regional income inequality. Aggregation is especially misleading in this instance because the Northeast shared very little in the economic development which took place within the rest of the country. Rather the tradeoff was between higher growth for the *Southeast* and stagnation (if not decline) in the *Northeast*. The Northeast bore the full burden of the economic costs that were entailed in maintaining Brazil's territorial unity.

In fact, the Northeast did not secede from the rest of Brazil. There were numerous complaints about the central government's discriminatory policies, and the Northeast's elites sometimes showed an awareness of the exchange-rate effects we have discussed.[84] Nevertheless, the last serious effort at secession occurred in 1849. Thereafter, the Northeast accepted the framework of a unified Brazil, and attempted to improve its lot within the system. Secessionist impulses may have been blunted by the fact that many of the region's difficulties came from the impersonal workings of the market mechanism rather than from overt and politicized instruments of 'internal colonialization'. In addition, Brazil's administrative and political elite had been socialized into taking a national rather than a regional view.[85] Finally, and not least important, the military failure of earlier attempts at secession also discouraged further efforts in that direction.

One last observation is pertinent here. Following major political changes in 1889, Brazil shifted from a centralized constitutional structure to one in which many administrative and fiscal functions were decentralized to the provincial level. It is worth noting that these constitutional changes did little to help the Northeast improve its economic situation. Administrative autonomy to bolster the sugar industry was of little avail in the face of the region's disadvantageous comparative-advantage and exchange-rate conditions. Thus, between 1889 and 1913, Brazil's income terms of trade in external sugar exports declined at a trend rate of 13.1 percent per annum.[86] Fiscal decentralization also failed to aid the Northeast in a significant way. The taxation (and foreign borrowing) capacity of the provincial governments in the Northeast was initially weak, for it rested on the (low) value of exports. And public-finance prospects did not brighten thereafter, for the subsequent decades saw a continuation of the Northeast's poor experience in international trade.[87] Economic resurgence in the Northeast required, at the least, measures to overcome the burdens from which the region's key commodities suffered because of their comparative disadvantage within Brazil. Administrative and fiscal decentralization altered neither the symptoms nor the causes of this situation.

Conclusions

The plight of the Northeast and the emergence of significant regional differentials in Brazilian economic development are not the result of twentieth-century industrialization, but date well back into the nineteenth century.[88] Exports were the main source of productivity increase and structural change in the Brazilian economy during the nineteenth century. The regional disparity stemmed from the fact that exports of coffee, in which the Southeast specialized, increased at a much higher rate than overseas sales of sugar and cotton, which were produced mainly in the Northeast. In practice, export growth was of strategic importance for economic development in nineteenth-century Brazil. Consequently, the Northeast's limited success in foreign trade also had far-reaching consequences for the expansion of socioeconomic infrastructure, urbanization, and industrialization in the region.

The poor performance of the Northeast's sugar and cotton exports, in turn, seems to have followed from a shift in Brazil's international comparative advantage. What should a country do when such a change in comparative advantage occurs? Clearly, resources should be reallocated to the activity which affords higher returns. To a limited extent this occurred in Brazil, particularly for slave labor. Capital and entrepreneurship, however, were often linked as joint inputs to land, which was not mobile. Moreover, in this instance, interactivity labor mobility required substantial geographical mobility. In the conditions of nineteenth-century Brazil, however, distant spatial movement involved high costs. Consequently, large-scale factor reallocation was impeded.

The predicament of the Northeast in the nineteenth century can thus be viewed as a case in which comparative advantage shifts, but in which the textbook assumptions of instantaneous and costless factor reallocation are not satisfied. At the same time, the country did have a unified foreign-exchange market. Consequently, Brazil's strong comparative advantage in coffee was reflected in a lower *mil-réis*/sterling exchange rate than would otherwise have prevailed. This lower conversion ratio, however, prevented ever-larger quantities of the Northeast's sugar and cotton exports from competing effectively on the world market. The coffee-dominated exchange rate also meant lower product prices and returns for the factors which remained in the Northeast's sugar and cotton. Finally, lower product prices led to parameter values at the micro level which reduced the possibilities for producers in the Northeast to escape from this situation by investing in modern technology.

Some of the conditions which have been proposed in *a priori* terms as causes of unequal regional development do not seem to have been important in the case of nineteenth-century Brazil. For example, there is little evidence of internal colonization, or of 'backwash effects' involving large-scale migration of capital and entrepreneurship from the poor to the rich region. However, other processes which have not received sufficient attention in the analysis of disparate regional development did operate, with pernicious interregional consequences. We have seen two such sets of conditions: the effects of the exchange-rate mechanism; and those which flowed from the fact that nineteenth-century Brazil did not satisfy the conditions of an optimum currency area. Each of these processes worsened the losses which originated from the shift in the country's comparative advantage. Under these conditions, the accidental circumstance of the spatial distribution of activities which ranked very differently in Brazil's comparative advantage led to a sequence whereby export expansion in one major region restricted exports and development in the other. Stated in such terms, the process may sound innocuous. But the consequences for economic development, regional inequality, and absolute poverty in Brazil were very great.

Our analysis of the Northeast's failure to achieve significant development during the nineteenth century also has implications for assessing the obstacles to economic progress in this historical context. It has sometimes been suggested that nineteenth-century Brazil would have achieved economic development more rapidly if its expansion path had been less oriented toward the growth of exports. The experience of the Northeast hardly supports that interpretation. As we have seen, the region's problem relative to the developing Southeast was not too high a level of exports, but rather one that was too low.[89] Similarly, our discussion of factor immobility and of regional differences in comparative advantage attributed considerable importance to land and climate, that is, to geographical conditions. But our analysis does not support interpretations of Brazil's regional disparity which have emphasized the fact that, like Argentina and Uruguay, the Southeast is closer to the temperate zone than is the Northeast. Coffee is of course just as much a tropical product as are cotton and sugar.

Finally, one by-product of this discussion is a recognition that standard analytical tools such as those employed in this chapter can explain an experience of unsuccessful economic development. This finding is no boon, however. If problems of economic retardation are amenable to social-science analysis, then we face a major intellectual challenge: attempting to isolate the conditions which prevented Brazil as a whole from achieving broad economic progress during the nineteenth century. Structural political factors are one obvious possibility. Such political constraints may have been either internal or external, and we will consider both in later chapters. Another possibility is that sociocultural conditions imparted serious rigidities to the economy, and prevented the market mechanism from operating effectively. Our discussion of the Northeast's experience during the nineteenth century raises scepticism about the general validity of such an interpretation. We were able to explain the emergence of significant regional differences in Brazilian development without invoking initial differences in 'values' as between the Northeast and Southeast.[90] On the contrary, we noted indications of significant freedom from supply rigidities, and of rational micro-level adjustment to the economic incentives which prevailed in the Northeast. However, the topic of sociocultural conditions as an obstacle to economic development in nineteenth century Brazil also raises other important issues, and requires a chapter for itself.

Notes

1 On the Northeast's poor development experience during the nineteenth century see, for example, Peter L. Eisenberg, *The Sugar Industry in Pernambuco: Modernization without Change, 1840–1910* (Berkeley: University of California Press, 1974). Rough estimates of per capita income growth in the Northeast and in the rest of Brazil between 1822 and 1913 are present in Nathaniel H. Leff, *Underdevelopment and Development in Brazil*, Vol. 1: *Economic Structure and Change* (London: Allen & Unwin, 1982), Chapter 3, Appendix II. Following the convention of the Brazilian Institute of Geography and Statistics, Brazil's various regions are defined in this chapter in the following way. The Northeast consists of Maranhão, Piauí, Ceara, Rio Grande do Norte, Paraíba, Pernambuco, Alagoas, Sergipe, Bahia, and Fernando Noronha; the North, of Amazonas, Pará, and the Territories; the Southeast, of Minas Gerais, Espírito Santo, Rio de Janeiro, and São Paulo; the South, of Paraná, Santa Catarina, and Rio Grande do Sul; and the Center–West, of Mato Grosso and Goiás.

2 For information on the Northeast at the end of our period, see Robert Levine, *Pernambuco in The Brazilian Federation, 1889–1937* (Stanford: Stanford University Press, 1978). Concerning the extent to which, in the middle of the twentieth century, Brazil's economic development was concentrated in the Southeast, see Stefan Robock, *Brazil's Developing Northeast* (Washington: The Brookings Institution, 1963).

3 See the materials presented in Jeffrey G. Williamson, 'Regional inequality and the Process of National Development: A Description of the Patterns,' *Economic Development and Cultural Change*, vol. 13, Part 2 (July 1965); Gunnar Myrdal, *Rich Lands and Poor* (New York: Harper, 1957), p. 170.

4 For an example of an historical study of regional inequalities, however, see Richard S. Eckaus, 'The North–South Differential in Italian Economic Development,' *Journal of Economic History*, vol. 20 (June 1961).

5 Between 1796 and 1808, the Northeast accounted for some 57 percent of Brazilian export receipts. This figure is from José Jobson de Andrade Arruda, 'O Brasil no Comércio Colonial, 1796–1808,' (Tese de Doutoramento, Universidade de São Paulo, 1972), p. 111. These figures relate to the turn of the century. By 1822, when Brazil achieved political independence, the Northeast may well have lost ground economically relative to the rest of Brazil.

6 Roberto C. Simonsen, *História Econômica do Brasil*, 4th edn São Paulo: Companhia Editora Nacional, 1962), pp. 375, 380. On the relative position of the Northeast see ibid., p. 294.

7 Computed from data which are presented in David Eltis, 'The Export of Slaves from Africa, 1821–1843,' *Journal of Economic History*, vol. 37 (June 1977), p. 416, Figure 8. Unfortunately, the printed version of this figure omitted the geographical indicators that were presented in the pre-publication, mimeographed version of the paper.

8 In 1823 the Northeast had approximately 54 percent of Brazil's stock of slaves; and the Southeast, 39 percent. See Table 2.4, below.

9 Computed from data which are presented in José Murilo de Carvalho, 'Elite and State Building in Imperial Brazil,' (PhD dissertation, Stanford University, 1974), p. 362.

10 See Table 2.4, below, and the discussion therein.

11 This figure is from J. Pandiá Calógeras, *A Política Monetária do Brasil* (trans. by Thomaz Newlands Neto from the 1910 edition of *La Politique Monetaire du Brésil*) (São Paulo: Companhia Editora Nacional, 1961), p. 179. A regional population breakdown for 1888 is not available, but the data of Table 2.4 (below) suggest that slaves probably constituted a higher proportion of the population of the Southeast than of the Northeast. Per-capita output levels may have been higher in the

Southeast than in the Northeast before the 1850s. However, the indicator of interregional slave movements was not available until the low-cost importation of slaves from Africa was stopped, in 1852.

12 On the failure of efforts to attract large-scale European immigration to the Northeast, see Eisenberg, *The Sugar Industry in Pernambuco*, op. cit., pp. 198–214.

13 Bainbridge Cowell, Jr, 'Cityward Migration in The Nineteenth Century: The Case of Recife, Brazil,' *Journal of Interamerican Studies and World Affairs*, vol. 17 (February 1975), p. 50. In the 1872 census, literacy rates in the Northeast were about as high as in the Southeast. This might be taken to imply that per capita income levels in the two regions were similar. However, in nineteenth-century Brazil, literacy depended on the distribution of income as well as on per capita income levels. Consequently, with a similar income distribution, literacy rates in the Northeast could approximate those of the Southeast even though average income levels were lower.

14 Leff, *Economic Structure and Change*, op. cit., Chapter 5.

15 Cf. a similar suggestion by Simonsen, *História Econômica*, loc cit. and pp. 405, 434–6. In the early nineteenth century Brazil's Southeast also exported some sugar; and following significant changes in relative prices during the twentieth century, the Southeast became a major producer of sugar and cotton. However, during most of the nineteenth century, Brazil's sugar and cotton were produced predominantly in the Northeast, while the Southeast specialized in coffee.

16 Exports of some other commodities produced in the Northeast, notably cocoa, expanded during the nineteenth century. However, as late as 1912–14, cocoa amounted to only 3 percent of Brazil's total export receipts. More generally, a rough computation (based on the assumption that all of Brazil's sugar, cotton, tobacco, and cocoa exports, and half of its leather exports came from the Northeast) indicates that the share of the Northeast in total Brazilian overseas export receipts fell from approximately 60 percent in 1821–23 to 36 percent in 1871–73 and 11 percent in 1912–14. The main factor in this decline was, as indicated in the text, the sharp drop in sugar and cotton exports.

17 These data on overseas sales of sugar and cotton do not give a complete picture of the growth of exports of these commodities in the Northeast; for an increasing part of the region's output was sold in the Brazilian Southeast. There are no reports, however, that the Northeast ran a continuing export surplus *vis-à-vis* the rest of the economy, with large net capital imports from the Southeast. Hence, a counterpart to those interregional sales from the Northeast must have been exports from the Southeast to the Northeast. Consequently, the data of Table 2.2 on the major export commodities of these regions do give an approximate idea of the *relative* rates of export growth in the Southeast and Northeast. The welfare effects of the Northeast's sugar exports to the Southeast are discussed later in this chapter.

18 See pp. 87–8 in Leff, *Economic Structure and Change*, op. cit., Chapter 5.

19 The figure for railway trackage in the Northeast is from Levine, *Pernambuco in The Brazilian Federation*, op. cit., p. 32.

20 Stanley J. Stein, *The Brazilian Cotton Manufacture* (Cambridge, Mass.: Harvard University Press, 1957), p. 21.

21 Computed from data in Richard Graham, *Britain and the Onset of Modernization in Brazil, 1850–1914*, (Cambridge University Press, 1968), p. 32, and from data on the regional distribution of Brazil's population. In 1872 the portion of the population which resided in the provincial capitals of the Northeast was some 10 percent lower than the comparable figure for the Southeast. That comparison, moreover, omits the population of Brazil's largest city, Rio de Janeiro (which was not a provincial capital). The large urban population of Rio de Janeiro partly reflected the fact that the city was the administrative and political capital of Brazil's central government, and hence does not indicate regional economic development *per se*. Still, from 1799

to 1864 the population of the city of Rio de Janeiro increased by perhaps a quarter of a million inhabitants. (See the estimates presented in Stein, *The Brazilian Cotton Manufacture*, op. cit., p. 8.) Only part of this large expansion was determined by the location of the capital in Rio. In fact, based on the growth of coffee exports and related activities, the city became Brazil's major economic and commercial center during the nineteenth century. Estimates of the growth of Recife during the nineteenth century are presented in Cowell, 'Cityward Migration,' op. cit., Table 1.

22 Eisenberg, *The Sugar Industry*, op. cit., p. 190, Table 32 and Table 30. Celso Furtado considered it plausible to suggest that the absolute level of per capita income in the Northeast may have fallen during the second half of the century. See his *Formação Econômica do Brasil*, 5th edn (Rio de Janeiro: Fundo de Cultura, 1963), pp. 117–18, 175. See also Jaime Reis, 'From Banguë to Usina: Pernambuco, 1850–1920,' in Kenneth Duncan and Ian Rutledge (eds) *Land and Labour in Latin America* (Cambridge University Press, 1977), p. 378.

23 In 1889, the British consul in Pernambuco reported that labor there was cheaper than anywhere in the world except Asia. This is cited in J. H. Galloway, 'The Last Years of Slavery on the Sugar Plantations of Northeast Brazil,' *Hispanic American Historical Review*, vol. 51 (November 1971), n. 54. For a general discussion of the grim conditions found in the Northeast at the end of the nineteenth century, see Levine, *Pernambuco*, op. cit., esp. Chapter 2.

24 Computed from figures of the British Board of Trade which are presented in D. C. M. Platt, *Latin America and British Trade, 1806–1914* (New York: Harper & Row, 1973), pp. 256–7.

25 These data are from Eisenberg, *The Sugar Industry*, p. 20. *Per capita* consumption of sugar in Great Britain increased 115 percent between 1832–42 and 1858–62; and by 280 percent from the same base period to 1878–88. These figures were computed from data in Albert H. Imlah, *Economic Elements in the Pax Britannica* (Cambridge, Mass.: Harvard University Press, 1958), p. 43.

26 See J. H. Galloway, 'The Sugar Industry of Pernambuco During the Nineteenth Century,' *Annals of the Association of American Geographers*, vol. 58 (June 1968), pp. 292–5. More generally, Brazil had ample land, and slaves were available in elastic supply from Africa until mid-century. Thereafter the country's large domestic agricultural sector contained considerable land and labor which could have been shifted to cotton and/or sugar production if returns had warranted. See Reis, 'From Banguë to Usina,' op. cit., p. 393; and Eisenberg, *The Sugar Industry*, op. cit., pp. 126–9, 195–7. Moreover, with favorable conditions in the product market, the supply of capital from internal and external sources would probably have been sufficiently elastic to permit growing output in the industry.

27 These data are from James A. Mann, *The Cotton Trade of Great Britain* (London, 1860; reprinted 1968), p. 43; from US government data cited in Albert Conrad *et al.*, 'Slavery as an Obstacle to Economic Growth in the United States: A Panel Discussion,' *The Journal of Economic History*, vol. 27 (December 1967), p. 529; and from Platt, *Latin America and British Trade*, op. cit., pp. 256–7.

28 Platt, *Latin America and British Trade*, op. cit., p. 257.

29 These data are from Eisenberg, *The Sugar Industry*, op. cit., p. 20.

30 Simonsen, *História Econômica*, op. cit., pp. 404–6, 434–6.

31 David Denslow, Jr, 'The Origins of Regional Economic Inequality in Brazil' (mimeo., University of Florida, 1978), p. 24.

32 Denslow. 'The Origins,' op. cit., p. 24.

33 R. Delson, 'Sugar Production for the Nineteenth-Century British Market: Rethinking the Roles of Brazil and the British West Indies' (mimeo., 1981).

34 Beet sugar accounted for some 7 percent of world sugar production in the 1840s; 27 percent in the 1860s; 42 percent in the 1870s; 58 percent in the 1880s; and 50 percent in the first decade of the twentieth century. These figures are from data compiled by Eisenberg, *The Sugar Industry*, op. cit., p. 20.

35   This decline appears in the data presented in Eisenberg, *The Sugar Industry*, op. cit., p. 20.

36   David Denslow, 'Sugar Production in Northeastern Brazil and Cuba, 1858–1908,' *Journal of Economic History*, vol. 35 (March 1975), p. 261. That discussion draws on detailed calculations presented in David Denslow, 'Sugar Production in Cuba and Northeast Brazil, 1850 to 1914, (mimeo., Yale University, 1971), Chapter 1. Denslow also notes that geographic distance and higher transport costs had not prevented Brazil from out-competing Cuba in the American market for coffee earlier in the nineteenth century.

37   Note 81, below, presents estimates of the extent of this diversion in the case of sugar from Pernambuco.

38   Eisenberg, *The Sugar Industry*, op. cit., pp. 25–9.

39   See the references cited in n. 26 above.

40   Denslow reaches a similar conclusion in his *Sugar Production in Cuba and Northeast Brazil*, op. cit., Chapter 1.

41   Mann, *The Cotton Trade of Great Britain*, op. cit., p. 86. See also Furtado, *A Formação Econômica*, op. cit., pp. 134–5.

42   Eisenberg, *The Sugar Industry*, op. cit., pp. 185–6, 190.

43   See Stein, *The Brazilian Cotton Manufacture*, op. cit., p. 221, n. 3, p. 222, n. 5; and David Denslow, 'As Origens da Desigualidade Regional no Brasil,' *Estudos Econômicos*, vol. 3 (1973), pp. 84–6.

44   Eisenberg, *The Sugar Industry*, op. cit., p. 48, 71, 33–4, 135–6.

45   See pp. 47–8 in Chapter 3, below. Using a different specification and data for the years 1857–1913, Denslow ('The Origins,' op. cit., p. 13) has estimated the short-run price elasticity of sugar supply in the Northeast to be 0.3, and the long-run elasticity to be 0.5. For cotton, he cites Gavin Wright's research which indicates a long-run price elasticity of approximately unity for Brazilian cotton. Wright's estimates are presented in his paper 'Cotton Competition and the Post-Bellum Recovery of The American South,' *Journal of Economic History* (September 1974), equation (17).

46   In his paper 'The Origins,' op. cit., David Denslow reports that in the 1906 harvest, the average cane yield in the Northeast was 52 tons per hectare. In Cuba, the average yield in the 1912–13 harvest was 47.6 tons per hectare. On the basis of his extensive knowledge of the sugar industry in both areas, Denslow apparently believes that these two years were sufficiently typical to permit comparisons.

47   Denslow, 'Sugar Production in Cuba and Northeast Brazil, 1850 to 1914,' op. cit., Chapters 1, 3, and Appendix A. Denslow's computations and discussion on lower productivity in the Northeast in relation to Cuba being offset by lower factor costs relate only to the period before 1884. For the subsequent decades, he has proposed an explanation of declining Brazilian exports which is discussed below.

48   See Stein, *The Brazilian Cotton Manufacture*, op. cit., p. 48. Simonsen has also stressed the importance of Brazil's technical lag behind the United States. He attributed 'the American victory' in the international cotton market mainly to Eli Whitney's invention (in 1793!) of the cotton gin. See Simonsen, *História Econômica*, op. cit., p. 370, n. 25. Whatever the causes of the productivity problem of cotton producers in the Northeast, they apparently did not derive from the technological or institutional 'learning curve' conditions which are emphasized by the infant-industry argument for subsidy. The volume of the Northeast's cotton exports rose sharply during the world cotton famine of the 1860s (see Table 23, above). However, Northeast producers did not achieve a lasting gain in their cost position. The improvement in international market share proved to be completely reversible, and by the late 1870s, Brazil's cotton exports had returned to the low level of the 1850s.

49   Eisenberg, *The Sugar Industry*, op. cit., pp. 40–2.

50 Eisenberg, *The Sugar Industry*, op. cit., pp. 41–4. See also Leff, *Economic Structure and Change*, op. cit., Chapter 7, pp. 139–40.

51 Accounts of this effort, which is strikingly contemporary in its self-conscious effort at economic (and social) salvation through technological modernization, are presented in Graham, *Britain and the Onset of Modernization in Brazil*, op. cit., pp. 149–58; Eisenberg, *The Sugar Industry*, op. cit., Chapter 5; and Galloway, 'The Sugar Industry of Pernambuco,' op. cit., pp. 300–2.

52 Levine, *Pernambuco*. op. cit., p. 26.

53 The figures which follow are from W. Arthur Lewis, *Aspects of Tropical Trade 1883–1965* (Stockholm: Almquist and Wiksell, 1969), p. 10.

54 Denslow, 'Sugar Production in Northeastern Brazil and Cuba,' op. cit., and 'Sugar Production in Cuba and Northeast Brazil,' op. cit., Chapter 1, 2, 4. He applied this analysis to the present problem in 'As Origens da Desigualidade,' op. cit., pp. 83–4, and in 'The Origins,' op. cit. In the latter paper (pp. 17–18) he makes clear that the conditions he discusses reflect 'the revolution in the technology of cane processing which began in the last years of the nineteenth century' (p. 17); and that these conditions did not affect Brazil's sugar exports 'until the late nineteenth century' (p. 18).

55 This well-established result of trade theory is presented in introductory textbooks on international economics. But because it is not an intuitive notion, we may avoid misunderstanding by using some clarifying notation here. Let C_{SB} denote the cost of producing sugar in Brazil; C_{AB}, the cost of producing alternative products in Brazil; C_{SO}, the cost of producing sugar in other countries; and C_{AO}, the cost of producing alternative products in other countries. Exportation of individual products in Brazil was determined by the ratio C_{SB}/C_{AB} – *not* by the ratio C_{SB}/C_{SO}. Consequently, the numerous studies which focus on the latter ratio are insufficient to explain the disparity in rates of export growth for different commodities in Brazil.

56 Such comparative analysis, moreover, may involve a serious measurement problem. International productivity comparisons are often based on the value of inputs per physical unit of output. If the input values are expressed in international currency to facilitate comparisons, their magnitude may be distorted by the exchange-rate effects which are discussed below. An overvalued exchange rate for the Northeast's sugar would overstate the value of the industry's inputs expressed in international currency and thus bias intercountry productivity comparisons.

57 Stein, *The Brazilian Cotton Manufacture*, op. cit., p. 47; and 'Evolution of Brazilian Cotton Plantations,' *Conjuntura Economica*, no. 5 (1970), p. 24.

58 Between 1822 and 1913, the sterling price of coffee relative to the sterling price of sugar in Brazil rose at an annual trend rate of 1.1 percent. The *t*-ratio for this trend coefficient is 8.46. The price of coffee relative to cotton also rose in Brazil during this period; but the trend has smaller magnitude (0.3 percent per annum) and a smaller *t*-ratio (2.08).

59 As a contemporary observer described this movement: 'The slaves have been drained into the Southern provinces for years. It is common to find three or four hundred of them on the Rio coffee plantations; rarely, there will be as many as a score on the sugar estates of Pernambuco or Pará.' See Herbert H. Smith, *Brazil, The Amazons and the Coast* (London, 1879), p. 470.

60 Transportation from Northeastern Brazil to the Southeast was usually by sea. From Recife to Rio de Janeiro, for example, this involved a trip of some 1200 miles. Another important element in the cost of the journey was incurred on the time-consuming and primitive transportation facilities between the hinterland and the ports.

61 Eisenberg, *The Sugar Industry*, op. cit., pp. 156–7.

62 Special low-quality accommodations were available for slaves shipped from the Northeastern ports to Rio de Janeiro; the charge for their transportation was approximately half the level of that for free passengers. I am indebted to Herbert Klein for this information.

63   Leff, *Economic Structure and Change*, op. cit., Chapter 7.
64   Information on the subsidization of European immigration to the Southeast is presented in Leff, *Economic Structure and Change*, op. cit., Chapter 4. As noted there, in the absence of subsidized overseas immigration, most of the Southeast's labor supply would probably have come initially from that region's domestic agricultural sector. Over time, however, people from the Northeast might have increasingly supplied the Southeast's labor demands, as did in fact happen from the 1930s onward. As noted in ibid., Chapter 4, the Northeast's landed interests did not restrict large-scale emigration from the Northeast to Brazil's Amazon region toward the end of the nineteenth century.
65   For example, on the United States, see Theodore W. Schultz, *Economic Organization and Agriculture* (New York: McGraw-Hill, 1953), Chapters 9 and 10.
66   For a detailed exposition of the concepts used here, See Michael Bruno, 'Domestic Resource Costs and Effective Protection: Clarification and Synthesis,' and Anne Krueger, 'Evaluating Restrictionist Trade Regimes: Theory and Measurement.' Both papers appear in the *Journal of Political Economy* (January 1972).
67   On the latter, see the spectral analysis of Alan Gleb, 'Coffee Prices and the Brazilian Exchange Rate,' *Oxford Economic Papers*, vol. 26 (March 1974).
68   Brazilian income and demand for imports were also higher because of coffee exports. In terms of the overall effects of coffee exports on the exchange rate, however, it should be remembered that the money supply was rarely determined by gold-standard considerations in nineteenth-century Brazil. Without the tax receipts derived from the foreign trade generated by coffee exports, the government would probably have expanded the money supply at a faster rate, leading to a higher *mil-réis*/sterling parity. Hence it is not likely that in the absence of coffee exports, the demand for imports would have shifted proportionately to the left. Moreover, coffee exports facilitated a larger volume of foreign-capital inflow than would otherwise have been possible. Apart from its effects on the capital account, capital imports were often oriented toward infrastructure facilities which subsequently increased the supply of foreign exchange on current account.
69   The years 1822–1913 were divided into two periods in order to avoid imposition of an assumption that the pertinent structural conditions did not change over this long time span. Choice of the year 1873 as the dividing point was to some extent arbitrary. The reasons for selection of that particular year are presented in Chapter 3, n. 13, below.
70   The large contribution of the covariance term for sugar in the earlier period is noteworthy. It probably reflects the importance of the sterling price of sugar in determining the annual sterling value of Brazil's sugar exports. Hence, given sugar's large share in Brazil's exports at that time, the sterling price of sugar was also a major determinant of the country's total foreign-exchange supply and exchange rate. Denslow ('The Origins,' op. cit., Table VI) attempted to develop additional econometric tests of the impact of coffee on the Brazilian exchange rate toward the end of the century. Unfortunately, his equations involve specification problems. Interpretation of his numerical results is also difficult because the meaning of his dependent variable – the sterling value of the Brazilian currency stock – is ambiguous. Additionally, Denslow's test was formulated in terms of the rate of growth (rather than the level) of coffee exports. Because of the comparative-advantage effects which are discussed below, however, the impact of coffee on the Brazilian exchange rate made itself felt via the annual *level* of sterling receipts derived from coffee exports.
71   There were sometimes slight disparities between the exchange rates in Rio de Janeiro and in Recife, but arbitrage of the foreign and the domestic banks kept these very small.
72   Depreciation of Brazil's unitary exchange rate, which occurred frequently in response to Brazil's long-term inflation, did not help sugar and cotton appreciably,

for they required a *mil-réis*/sterling exchange rate that was permanently lower than coffee. After the analysis of this section was completed, I learned that Jonathan V. Levin had earlier discussed some effects of a unitary exchange rate on exports under conditions of factor immobility. See his *The Export Economies: Their Pattern of Development in Historical Perspective* (Cambridge, Mass.: Harvard University Press, 1961), p. 275.

73 Under a multiple exchange-rate system, one exchange rate would have been given to coffee, and another (higher) *mil-réis* parity would have been given to exporters of sugar and cotton.

74 The discussion that follows here draws on theoretical analysis which is presented in R. A. Mundell 'A Theory of Optimum Currency Areas,' *American Economic Review*, vol. 51 (September 1961); and Tibor Scitovsky, *Money and the Balance of Payments* (Chicago: Rand McNally, 1968), Chapter 8.

75 See, for example, Galloway, 'The Last Years,' op. cit., n. 49. On higher interest rates in the Northeast than in the Southeast, see Leff, *Economic Structure and Change*, op. cit., Chapter 4, pp. 48–9, and the references cited there.

76 Interregional differentials in interest rates may of course have been a way around exchange-rate fixity. Such asset-market adjustments had the same deflationary bias as the conditions discussed in the text.

77 See, for example, the 1875 statement of the British Consul in Pernambuco: 'The immense number of people without a trade or ostensible means of living is truly astonishing.' (cited in Galloway, 'The Last Years,' op. cit., n. 46). More generally, on underemployment in the region, see Eisenberg, *The Sugar Industry*, op. cit., pp. 194–7. Underemployment in the Northeast seems to have reflected the deflationary conditions discussed in the text rather than generalized excess supply of labor. Thus increased demand for workers in railway construction during the late 1850s led to higher wages, as did the cotton boom of the 1860s. Wages in the Northeast were downwardly flexible from peak levels which they reached during such booms, but for obvious reasons, wages were rigid downwards at the subsistence levels.

78 For a discussion of the possibility of mechanisms which may make for convergence and eliminate regional inequalities, see Williamson, 'Regional Inequality,' op. cit.

79 On these last points, see Stanley J. Stein, *Vassouras: A Brazilian Coffee County* (Cambridge, Mass.: Harvard University Press, 1957), p. 64; and Eisenberg, *The Sugar Industry*, op. cit., pp. 222–3.

80 See Levine, *Pernambuco in The Brazilian Federation*, passim. On policy efforts during the twentieth century, see Albert O. Hirschman, *Journeys Toward Progress* (New York: Doubleday, 1963), Chapter 1.

81 During the 1860s, domestic shipments accounted for 21 percent of the value of sugar exports from Pernambuco, the largest sugar-producing province. For the 1870s and 1880s, the figures are 19 and 22 percent, respectively. At the end of our period, in the years 1906–10, the domestic market accounted for 85 percent of Pernambuco's shipments. These figures are from Eisenberg, *The Sugar Industry*, op. cit.. p. 17.

82 See pp. 73–4 in Chapter 4, below.

83 On industrial development in the Southeast at this time, see Warren Dean, *The Industrialization of São Paulo, 1880–1945* (Austin: University of Texas Press, 1969), Chapters 1 and 4.

84 Eisenberg, *The Sugar Industry*, op. cit., p. 18.

85 See E. S. Pang and R. L. Seckinger, 'The Mandarins of Imperial Brazil,' *Comparative Studies in Society and History*, vol. 14 (March 1972); and José Murilo de Carvalho, 'Elite and State Building in Imperial Brazil,' op. cit., Chapters 1–3.

86 The income terms of trade (V_x/p_m) were computed using the British export price index as a rough proxy for a price index of Brazil's imports. The *t*-ratio for the trend term cited in the text is 6.53. The precipitous decline in the value of the Northeast's overseas exports between 1889 and 1913 reflects the diversion of sugar output or sale in the internal market. The effects of such sales on welfare levels in the

Northeast are discussed in the text, above. Between 1889 and 1913, Brazil's barter terms of trade (P_x/p_m) in sugar fell at an annual trend rate of 1.9 percent $(t=3.46)$.

87   On the experience of the region's largest province, see Levine, *Pernambuco*, op. cit., Chapters 6 and 7, and pp. 187–92. Pernambuco did not borrow abroad until 1906, when it contracted a foreign loan of $4.8 million. In 1913, Pernambuco's foreign debt stood at $11.3 million (ibid., p. 189). By contrast, the Southeast provinces with their more favorable economic conditions, were able to borrow abroad much earlier and on a much larger scale following the fiscal decentralization of the new constitution.

88   The North–South disparity in Italy also seems to be a case where regional inequality antedates, and therefore cannot be attributed wholly to, modern industrialization. See Eckaus, 'The North–South Differential in Italian Economic Development,' op. cit., pp. 300, 315–17.

89   Chapter 4 below, considers in greater detail the relevance of a 'dependency' interpretation of nineteenth-century Brazil's economic experience.

90   For a similar view which minimizes the importance of (initial) differences in 'values' in the disparate regional development of Colombia, see Albert O. Hirschman, *The Strategy of Economic Development* (New Haven: Yale University Press, 1958), pp. 185–6; and Alvaro Lopez Toro, 'Migración y Cámbio Social en Antioquia durante el Siglo XIX,' *Demografia y Economía*, vol. 5 (1968).

3
Sociocultural Conditions

Background of the Discussion

Anyone seeking a general explanation of Brazil's economic retardation soon encounters one interpretation which has had a special attraction for some observers and social scientists. Social structure and cultural norms in Brazil seem to have been very different from those of, say, the United States during the nineteenth century. Accordingly, socio-cultural conditions in Brazil have sometimes been viewed as a major underlying cause of the country's poorer economic experience.

Explanations of economic underdevelopment in such institutional terms have been common, both for Latin America in general and for Brazil in particular.[1] Some interpretations have stressed the deficiencies for development of a social structure rigidly cast in a two-class, master–slave mold, with no middle social stratum. Other perspectives have focused on Brazilian culture and values, which are alleged to have been inimical in some ways to economic rationality. This approach suggests that psychocultural imperatives led to behavior in which Brazilians did not respond effectively to economic conditions. Such behavior would result in what might be characterized (in narrow economic terms) as rigidities. As a consequence, Brazil would have suffered from both static allocational inefficiencies and intertemporal dynamic losses. Brazil's Iberian and Catholic cultural heritage – which seems to have been very different from, for example, Max Weber's *Protestant Ethic and The Spirit of Capitalism* – has sometimes been proposed as the distortion which hampered the country's economic development. The culture and values which emerged in a seigneurial, 'tropical' society like nineteenth-century Brazil have also been cited in this context.

An interpretation along such lines may (or may not) have a certain *a priori* appeal for students of Brazil's economic history.[2] But in any case, in order to take such an approach seriously, we must avoid a simplistic view of the relation between sociocultural conditions and the economy. First, it is essential to eschew reification. Terms like 'culture' or 'social conditions' do not indicate entities which constitute a reality in themselves, but rather refer to generalized, observed behavior of individuals. Further, social structure and values in nineteenth-century Brazil were obviously part of a larger political and economic reality.

Also, sociocultural and economic conditions were clearly related in a reciprocal rather than in a unidirectional manner. Finally, the question of possible sociocultural constraints on economic development is obviously not an either/or issue. A more fruitful approach is to consider the areas of behavior in which sociocultural conditions seem to have impeded economic progress in nineteenth-century Brazil, as well as those where they did not.

We will begin our inquiry by considering a central issue: to what extent did sociocultural constraints prevent producers in nineteenth-century Brazil from allocating their resources in a manner which responded to changes in price and market conditions? Economic development requires more than a market mechanism in which production adjusts flexibly to changing relative prices. Because of conditions such as the existence of public goods, economic externalities, and imperfect knowledge, even a well-functioning market mechanism does not assure a pattern of resource allocation which is socially optimal.[3] Indeed, if producers and consumers respond with admirable microeconomic rationality but the market gives the wrong price signals, economic efficiency is reduced rather than enhanced. Notwithstanding these limitations of the market mechanism, however, it would also be a mistake to underestimate the importance of price-responsive behavior. Economic development will usually proceed more rapidly in a country where producers increase output of a product when its relative price rises, and reduce output when the product's relative price falls than in a country where supply curves for individual products are vertical.

Finally, this discussion is also relevant in a broader intellectual context. In the early postwar period, interpretations of economic underdevelopment often attributed considerable importance to cultural constraints which might be present in less-developed societies. Subsequent research disclosed evidence of microeconomic rationality on the part of producers in widely diverse 'traditional societies' in recent decades.[4] However, it is not clear that similar market-responsive behavior also prevailed in such societies during earlier periods. Two separate issues are raised here. First, there is a methodological question: to what extent are economic models which are predicated on the assumption of economic rationality relevant for analyzing the economic history of less-developed countries? In addition, there is a substantive issue: to what extent can the poor economic experience of the less-developed countries in earlier historical periods be attributed to sociocultural conditions which constrained the operation of an effective price mechanism, and thus obstructed an economically rational allocation of resources?

One way to help resolve these questions is to examine available empirical materials for evidence of market responsiveness. As a step in this direction, this chapter presents some econometric materials which test the hypothesis that Brazil's export supply was responsive to changes in relative prices during the nineteenth century. This material is germane to the general discussion, for unlike the case in many underdeveloped countries, the entrepreneurs in Brazil's export activities were native-born rather than foreigners. We then consider in broader terms the place of sociocultural conditions in both Brazil's economic experience and in the country's economic historiography.

Testing for Price Responsiveness

Data are available on the annual export quantum and on the unit value (henceforth referred to as price) of Brazil's major export products from 1822 to 1913.[5] The availability of these data permits the estimation of price-response equations for individual commodities. These equations, in turn, enable us to ascertain the degree to which the producers of Brazil's exports adjusted their output in response to changing relative prices during the nineteenth century.

Before proceeding to specify regression equations and estimate price elasticities of supply, however, we must confront some potential problems posed by the data. First comes the obvious question concerning their reliability. Fortunately, econometric theory indicates that statistical conclusions can be drawn from parameter estimates even though the underlying observations may clearly be subject to errors in measurement.[6] Errors of measurement in the dependent variable would not bias the parameter estimates, but would increase their variance and thus lead to an understatement of the true t-ratios. If there are errors in measurement in the independent variables, the effects on the parameter estimates depend on the ratio of the variance of the errors relative to the variance of the true independent variable. If this ratio is very small, the parameter estimates are unaffected. If the ratio is large, the parameter estimates – in the present case, the supply elasticities – are biased *downward*. Thus, the possible presence of errors of measurement does not invalidate our tests, but rather tends to bias the estimates against accepting the hypothesis of price-responsive behavior.

Another potential problem is posed by the fact that the data available do not include estimates of the annual stock of trees used to produce non-perennial crops like coffee and cacao. Accurate specification of the supply-adjustment process for such commodities requires observations of the number of trees (or of the area allocated to them).[7] Because such data are not available for nineteenth-century Brazil, the parameters of price-response equations for the non-perennial commodities cannot be estimated. In the present context, however, this omission does not entail as great a loss as might first appear. Our purpose here is not to explain Brazilian export supply, but rather to test for the presence of price-responsive behavior in the Brazilian economy during the nineteenth century. Hence, the fact that coffee was a major source of Brazilian export earnings does not confer special importance on that particular commodity. Moreover, by all accounts, coffee production was responsive to price incentives in nineteenth-century Brazil.[8] The question is whether such economic behavior was general or whether it was characteristic only of a special group, the coffee-planters. To answer that question, our focus on a diverse and wide-ranging set of commodities – cotton, sugar, leather, tobacco, and rubber – is meaningful.[9]

One standard model which economists have used to estimate the the parameters of supply-response behavior is not very helpful in the present context.[10] That model involves regressing the annual export quantity of each product on lagged quantity and relative-price terms. The equation also includes a trend term, in reflection of the long-term increase of population and of complementary factors in Brazil between 1822 and 1913. This specification captures the impact of the outward shift of production-possibility curves on the growth of Brazil's exports during this long period.

In preliminary work for the present study, regression equations of this form were in fact estimated, and the results were consistent with price-responsive behavior. But a definite conclusion on this point was not possible; for, as might be expected, the trend terms account for much of the goodness-of-fit in such equations for the growth of Brazil's export supply. Interpretation of the trend terms presents difficulties, however, in the present context, where we are testing for evidence of responsiveness to relative-price changes. The coefficients on the trend terms may reflect nothing more than exogenous growth of population in the course of the nineteenth century. Alternatively, the trends may also mirror a true economic adjustment, such as factor reallocation to take advantage of the opportunities in individual products.[11] This ambiguity constitutes an obvious problem here, where the purpose of the analysis is to draw clear-cut conclusions concerning the existence of price-responsive behavior. Consequently, an alternative model was utilized which focuses more directly on the presence or absence of price-responsive behavior.

The Model

In order to eliminate the effects of trend from the analysis, the observations for each export quantum series were detrended. That is, a logarithmic trend equation was fitted to each series, and the exports of each product were then expressed as the annual deviation of the series from its logarithmic trend. The detrended quantities for each export commodity are denoted $q_{i,t}$.

With the $q_{i,t}$ specified as the dependent variable, the model utilized is a modification of Marc Nerlove's well-known adaptive-expectations model.[12] The general hypothesis tested is that producers respond to changes in market conditions with changes in their production decisions. Specifically, if the *mil-réis* price of an individual (*i*th) commodity is expected to rise relative to the price of other products which use similar inputs, producers will expand production of the *i*th commodity. By the same token, if producers expect the price of the *i*th commodity to fall relative to the price of the (*j*th) product with which it competes for factors, producers will shift to the *j*th product, and output of commodity *i* will contract. As this discussion indicates, the model hypothesizes that production decisions are made in function of *expected* prices. The appendix to this chapter presents details on estimation procedures and on the technique which was used to generate the expected-price series for each commodity (p_i^e) and for its closest substitute in production (p_j^e).

The test we are posing, then, is a stringent one. Can annual deviations from trend of the individual export commodities' quantum be explained as a function of expected relative prices? To complete the specification of our regression equation, we add a constant and a stochastic term. And to permit ready interpretation of the coefficients on the price terms as elasticities, these variables are specified in natural logarithms. Thus the basic model to be estimated for each commodity in order to test for price responsiveness is:

$$q_{i,t} = a_0 + a_1 \ln p_{i,t}^e + a_2 \ln p_{j,t}^e + u_{i,t} \qquad (1)$$

If Brazilian producers did in fact adjust their output in response to changes in expected prices, this behavior would be reflected in positive parameter estimates for a_1, and negative parameter estimates for a_2. Both coefficients should of course be statistically different from zero. By contrast, the existence of supply rigidities would be reflected in insignificant parameter estimates and a poor statistical fit for the individual equations.

Before proceeding to estimation of the supply-response parameters, we must consider some possible problems with this specification. It would obviously be preferable to specify changes in the acreage under cultivation rather than in the export quantum as the dependent variable in these supply-response equations. This is because acreage rather than quantity is the producer's policy instrument; and quantities may vary with changes in yields (quantities per acre) as well as with variations in acreage cultivated. As mentioned earlier, annual data on acreage by crop are not available for nineteenth-century Brazil. But in any case, the failure to specify acreage should not bias our parameter estimates. Weather conditions were probably the main determinant of fluctuations in yields. However, weather was presumably a random element, and consequently would enter the stochastic term of the equations estimated.

The possibility of simultaneous-equations bias poses another potential problem. The dependent variable in equation (1) is the annual deviation from trend in the quantum *exported* rather than in the total quantum *produced*. (Data for the latter are not available.) Total production would of course include the portion of each commodity's output that was consumed within Brazil rather than exported. If the portion consumed domestically were jointly determined with the lagged price changes which underly our p^e variables, the parameter estimates of (1) would be biased. That condition does not seem to have prevailed, however. Prices of Brazil's individual export commodities, each of which constituted only part of total export receipts, changed at different rates during the nineteenth century. Moreover, each export product accounted for only a small share of domestic income. Hence, it is unlikely that changes in the total of current internal demand for individual exportable commodities were determined by lagged changes in the prices of individual products. The fact that our dependent variable relates to export supply, while our explanatory variables relate to total production does, however, have another statistical consequence. The goodness-of-fit will be reduced in the equations for products in which internal consumption accounted for a non-negligible share of total production. Leather, tobacco, and, later in the century, cotton are examples of such products in the Brazilian context.

Simultaneity bias may also arise from another possible source. Price and quantity might be jointly determined because Brazil had a large share in the world market. That condition did not in fact prevail for four of the five commodities in our sample; consequently, price was determined independently of Brazil's exports. The only exception is rubber. However, the possibility of simultaneity bias in rubber is reduced by the fact that the price variables reflect lagged rather than current values. Preliminary estimation of the model indicated the presence of serial correlation in the residuals. The Cochrane–Orcutt transformation was therefore employed to obtain efficient parameter estimates. This procedure also provides us with estimates of the first-order autoregressive term, ρ for each equation.

Note, finally, that because of the procedure used to generate the series for expected prices, our analysis deals with the years 1824–1913. Estimating a single equation for that entire period, however, would imply the unrealistic assumption that the model's structural parameters did not change over the century. To avoid imposing such restrictions on the data, the observations were divided at 1873, and separate equations were fitted for the years 1824–73 and 1874–1913. This division is to some extent arbitrary. But it does permit us to estimate separate equations for the earlier and later periods, between which structural shifts may have occurred which altered supply-response behavior in Brazil.[13]

Evidence of Price Responsiveness

Table 3.1 shows the parameter estimates and summary statistics obtained from estimating our model of supply-response behavior. Since we have five commodities and two time periods, the result of ten equations are presented. Recalling our earlier discussion, the parameter a_1 shows the response of deviations from the trend in a given

Table 3.1 *Parameter Estimates and Summary Statistics for Equations Estimating the Price-Responsiveness of Producers in Brazil's Five Major Perennial Export Commodities, 1824–1913*

Product and Period	Parameter estimate for:			
	a_1 Own-Price Response	a_2 Cross-Price Response	p	R^2
Cotton, 1824–73	.130	.261	.310	.78
	(9.02)	(4.26)	(2.30)	
1874–1913	−.815	.069	.272	.22
	(2.40)	(2.22)	(1.79)	
Sugar, 1824–73	.032	−.196	.421	.53
	(2.61)	(3.81)	(3.28)	
1874–1913	.680	−.278	.389	.36
	(2.90)	(2.31)	(2.67)	
Leather, 1824–73	−.286	.032	.575	.44
	(1.96)	(0.61)	(4.97)	
1874–1913	.082	−.171	.678	.60
	(2.06)	(1.54)	(5.83)	
Tobacco, 1824–73	.016	−.529	.496	.27
	(1.58)	(2.04)	(4.04)	
1874–1913	.367	−.326	−.178	.27
	(3.45)	(2.97)	(1.14)	
Rubber, 1829–73	.419	−.176	.808	.72
	(3.24)	(3.00)	(9.21)	
1874–1913	.150	−.048	.586	.42
	(1.64)	(1.79)	(4.58)	

Notes: The dependent variable in each equation is the annual deviation of the individual product from its long-term logarithmic trend during the period specified. These equations were estimated using the Cochrane–Orcutt transformation. The absolute value of the t-ratio for each parameter estimate is presented in parentheses. With a normal distribution and thirty degrees of freedom, the critical value of t for significance at the 90 percent level in a one-tailed test is 1.310; and at the 95 percent level, 1.697. As noted in n. 13, however, because of the estimation procedures used, these t-ratios are only approximate. Information concerning the procedures used to generate the expected price series is presented in the Appendix to this chapter. The jth products specified in each equation are listed in n. 14.

commodity's export supply to changes in the commodity's own expected price. Price-responsive behavior would be reflected in own-price coefficients which are positive and significant.[14] Estimation also provides parameter estimates for a_2. These cross-price coefficients show the short-term supply response of each product to changes in the expected price of the commodity with which it competed for factor supplies.[15] Price-responsive behavior with respect to this alternative product would be shown in cross-price coefficients which are negative and statistically different from zero.

Table 3.1 indicates a clear pattern of price-responsive behavior. The R^2's of most equations indicate a relatively good fit. This finding is particularly noteworthy because the dependent variable is expressed in deviations from trend, and because the Cochrane–Orcutt transformation has eliminated the statistical impact of serial correlation.[16] Also, the few cases where the statistical fit of the equations is poor (e.g. cotton in the period of 1874–1913) are explicable in a straightforward manner. By the 1870s, Brazil had developed a cotton textile industry, which purchased an increasingly large share of the country's raw cotton production. The level of the country's annual exports and the *mil-réis* price of cotton were thus significantly affected by domestic demand pressures, including those generated by the country's internal inflation. For this reason, our use of the export quantum data to proxy for total production involves the distortion which we noted in our earlier discussion.

The parameter estimates for a_1 and a_2 also confirm this general pattern of price-responsive behavior. Eight of the ten parameter estimates of a_1 are positive and larger than their standard errors. (The 'anomalies' are cotton in the later period, and leather in the earlier period.) We have already noted the importance of domestic demand pressures for Brazilian cotton. And because of leather's joint-product association with beef, a similar export response to domestic demand expansion probably also prevailed in that commodity. Further, the hypothesis that Brazilian producers adjusted their output rationally to changes in expected prices posits that the estimates for the a_2 term will be significantly negative. In fact, eight of the ten estimates for a_2 are negative and larger than their standard errors.

Taken together, these statistical findings indicate a pattern that is fairly consistent. Similarly, the results of another (simpler) model which was estimated with these data lead to the same conclusion. As discussed in the Appendix, those results also confirm the presence of price-responsive behavior in these activities. This econometric evidence, which indicates that export producers in nineteenth-century Brazil adjusted their output in response to relative-price changes, could not have been predicted with certainty *a priori*.

In several instances the supply-response coefficients shown in Table

3.1 are relatively small in magnitude. Thus nine of the sixteen coefficients which are larger than their standard errors and of the correct sign have an absolute value less than .2. These values do not necessarily indicate weak responsiveness to price changes, however. In some cases, they reflect the special form of equation (1), and the fact that the dependent variable is specified in terms of the annual deviations from long-term trend (see below). Further, factor endowments and the range of actual prices must also be taken into account. These may have led producers in some activities to optimize with a corner solution, so that supply of individual commodities varied little with price changes. An example of such behavior is cotton production in the South of the United States during the ante-bellum period. There, producers were very much oriented to price and market conditions. But although cotton production in the United States increased remarkably in response to favorable long-term opportunities, it was not responsive to relative-price changes on an annual basis.[17]

In Brazil, too, differential trends in rates of output growth were also a major feature of microeconomic adjustment to market incentives. As explained earlier, in order to provide an unambiguous test of short-term price-responsive behavior, we eliminated long-term trend terms from our regression equations. However, that methodological procedure also suppressed a key aspect of market adjustment in nineteenth-century Brazil. For in fact the production-possibility curves in different activities did not shift outward at a uniform rate, in reflection simply of exogenous population growth. Rather, the trends in the export quanta for individual products varied considerably, apparently in response to differences in rates of return. Table 3.2 presents data on the trend rates of growth for Brazil's eight major export commodities. The table includes the data for tree crops such as

Table 3.2 *Long-Term Trend Rates of Growth in the Export Quanta of Eight Commodities in Nineteenth-Century Brazil*

Product	Period	Quantum Exported (percent)	Product	Period	Quantum Exported (percent)
Cotton	1822–73	2.5	Tobacco	1822–73	3.0
	1874–1913	−1.9		1874–1913	1.1
Sugar	1822–73	2.2	Cacao	1822–73	3.2
	1874–1913	−6.4		1874–1913	5.5
Coffee	1822–73	5.3	Rubber	1828–73	10.0
	1874–1913	3.8		1874–1913	5.7
Leather	1822–73	2.5	Erva[a] maté	1831–74	6.4
	1874–1913	2.0		1874–1913	5.3

[a] Erva maté is a South American tea.

coffee and cacao; and the figures are arrayed in descending order of importance of each commodity to Brazil's aggregate export receipts at the beginning of the period.

As Table 3.2 indicates, the quantum trends in Brazil's diverse export activities during the nineteenth century trend coefficients were very different from the country's overall rate of population increase (approximately 1.8 percent per annum). In addition, the trends (positive or negative) in the different export commodities varied markedly between activities. This pattern of differential rates of expansion suggests that resources were not allocated to individual activities in a simple autoregressive or vegetative manner. The underlying reason for this pattern of differential rates of long-term trend growth may well have been differential profitability.

In fact, the more profitable commodities (e.g. coffee) expanded at rates that were much higher than those of activities which are known to have suffered economic distress (e.g. sugar). Similarly, new export products, such as rubber and erva maté, emerged and grew at an especially rapid pace during the nineteenth century. Coming together with the positive covariance between price and supply, the differential quantum trends shown in Table 3.2 led to major changes in the composition of Brazil's exports during the nineteenth century. In 1821–23, coffee, cacao, rubber and erva maté had accounted for some 20 percent of Brazil's export receipts. In 1912–14, the figure had risen to 84 percent. Further, this picture of rational economic adjustment by means of disparate quantum trends persists if we exclude coffee (which may be dismissed as a special case), and focus only on cacao, rubber, and erva maté. The producers of these three products, located in diverse regions throughout the country, are not as well-known for their enterprising behavior as was Brazil's coffee elite, who were renowned for such behavior. Nevertheless, the output of cacao, rubber, and erva maté increased so dramatically that the share of these products in Brazil's export receipts rose from approximately 1 percent at the beginning of the period to 24 percent at its end.[18]

By the nature of the documentation which has survived, the evidence which we have examined for price-responsiveness in Brazil during the nineteenth century relates to the export activities rather than to the domestic agricultural sector of the economy. However, one cannot take optimizing microeconomic behavior for granted even in a country's export sector. Thus, some theoretical models of international trade in less-developed countries during the post-Second World War period find it plausible to assume that supply rigidities are prevalent in the export sector.[19] More generally, however, evidence is available on the presence of price-responsive behavior in the domestic sector of Brazil's economy in the nineteenth century. Thus, when relative-price conditions offered favorable economic incentives, factor supplies moved from the domestic agricultural sector to the country's export activities. Similarly, empirical information on monetary conditions in Brazil also indicates a high degree of market responsiveness. The monetized sector encompassed many activities in Brazil's domestic sector as well as activities in the external sector. And here, too, Brazilians displayed swift adjustment behavior.[20] Similarly, outside of Brazil's export activities, workers were also highly mobile both geographically and between occupations.[21]

Structural conditions such as transportation costs and the need for capital and complementary resources obviously affected the extent of this mobility. But what is important in the present context is that the constraints stressed in sociocultural interpretations of economic underdevelopment, for example, 'tradition' or social and geographical ties, apparently did not stand in the way of an economically rational allocation (or reallocation) of resources.[22] The contrast here is with some other pre-industrial societies, where kin, caste, values, or feudal-type restrictions may seriously inhibit economically rational responses to changing economic incentives. That does not seem to have been a general feature of the economy in Brazil during the nineteenth century. Describing Brazilian society at the beginning of the nineteenth century, an eminent historian has spoken of an 'immense inorganic segment of the community made up of rootless individuals'.[23] This description does not suggest a situation in which feudal social structure or organic cultural values impeded economically rational allocation of resources.

Price Responsiveness and Development Failure

The materials just discussed add to the extensive evidence which has accumulated on the presence of price-responsive behavior in underdeveloped countries. Perhaps the only novel feature is that our statistical results relate to the nineteenth rather than to the twentieth century.[24] Some observers may consider it axiomatic that *homo economicus* is present in all eras and locales.[25] However, many social scientists may consider it more plausible to view underdeveloped countries as characterized by pervasive rigidities due to sociocultural conditions.[26] Hence it is helpful to approach the question of possible sociocultural distortions in Brazil's economic experience with empirical information rather than with *a priori* convictions.

It is important to recognize that although Brazilian producers may have responded to changing relative prices, Brazil did not achieve rapid economic development during the nineteenth century. Economic development evidently requires more than supply responsiveness. In general terms, a number of conditions may prevent a country from enjoying economic progress even though its economic agents respond admirably to changes in relative prices at the microeconomic level. For example, because of well-known conditions of private market failure, the price system may provide signals which are distorted from a social viewpoint. Several instances of such market failure are apparent in Brazil during the nineteenth century. Thus, distortions in land and credit markets permitted local oligopsony in the demand for free labor. External economies and diseconomies were also present. Thus, fertility rates in nineteenth-century Brazil may have reflected behavior that was rational for individuals, but involved social diseconomies. Similarly, economic externalities helped delay the extension of Brazil's railway system.

Further, in cases where market distortions led to socially inappropriate prices, optimizing behavior at the micro level would not induce efficient development. Following standard welfare theory, an improved outcome would depend on the government's intervening in ways that would correct the distorted price signals or their effects. The unhappy experience of the Northeast illustrates the need for such 'macro rationality': a society's capacity to resolve structural problems whose modification is beyond the scope of individual economic agents. And as that experience demonstrates, Brazilian governments were not always able to act in a manner that corrected market imperfections. Chapter 5, below, focuses on government behavior and its limitations in nineteenth-century Brazil.

As this discussion suggests, microeconomic rationality is not a sufficient condition for a country to achieve rapid economic development. But by the same token, a low rate of economic development does not necessarily indicate the absence of optimizing economic behavior. In addition to this point in logic, the empirical materials which we discussed above are also relevant. Those, too, suggest the need to reconsider any preconception that because of culture or social structure, Brazilians did not follow optimizing behavior at the microeconomic level. Such a reconsideration is especially necessary because observers have sometimes been predisposed to attribute negative features of Brazil's economic experience to sociocultural conditions. That approach, however, may lead to misinterpretations; for what may in fact be observed are rational economic responses to relevant structural conditions.

Sociocultural Conditions and Brazil's Economic Retardation

In a number of important instances, some earlier interpretations seem to have overemphasized the role of Brazilian values in slowing the country's economic development. For example, rates of saving and investment in nineteenth-century Brazil were relatively low. This behavior has often been attributed to Brazilian values, which allegedly placed a heavy stress on immediate (and conspicuous) consumption. A comparative perspective, however, helps in evaluating this interpretation. British capitalists, too, invested relatively little in Brazil until the end of the nineteenth century.[27] The behavior of these foreign capitalists was not constrained by Brazil's cultural norms. And the fact that foreign entrepreneurs nevertheless invested so little in the country suggests that they were responding to unfavorable structural conditions, such as low (private) returns to capital. Such a situation would also account for low rates of saving and investment by Brazilians.

Low marginal returns in many activities would also help explain another aspect of Brazilian behavior which has often been ascribed to the country's 'mentality': a disinclination to undertake investments which involved a relatively long time-horizon. Such behavior is eminently rational, however, under conditions in which risks are greater for longer-term investments, but returns do not increase commensurately. We have already noted the effects of Brazil's chronic (but variable) inflation in raising the *ex ante* uncertainty surrounding long-term lending and investment decisions.[28] Other historical information also supports an interpretation which is formulated in terms of risk and return conditions. Note that in cases where relatively high returns were available, Brazilians did invest in projects with long gestation periods. Thus coffee trees do not begin to yield significant returns until five years after planting, and cacao trees, until eight years. Nevertheless, Brazilians committed large long-term resources to those activities when returns appeared attractive.

Other behavior also raises doubts concerning any presumption that culture and values led Brazilians to preferences characterized by extreme risk aversion. For example, in the first half of the century, planters in the Northeast were so keen to obtain the higher returns offered by the export crops that they neglected production of foodstuffs. As a consequence, provincial governments repeatedly had to enjoin the planters to produce a more balanced portfolio of products.[29] (Note that the plantation labor force in the Northeast during that period consisted mostly of slaves. Hence the planters had to internalize the costs of higher food prices due to possible supply shortages.) And more widely in the country, the shift of Brazilian producers from subsistence to export production during the nineteenth century suggests a like conclusion concerning risk aversion. The issue in the present context is not the advisability of this shift; specialization in the export activities entailed accepting the risks of the international market and, often, the hazards of monoculture as well. What is relevant here is that these actions do not suggest attitudes of extreme risk aversion.

Our discussion thus far has focused on saving and investment behavior. Similarly, sociocultural conditions have sometimes been given too prominent a role in interpreting important labor-market phenomena in nineteenth-century Brazil. For example, the demand for slaves in nineteenth-century Brazil, and variations in price for different age and sex groups of slaves can be explained in terms of net returns to the planters.[30] It is not necessary to invoke non-economic considerations such as the Brazilian elite's desire for dependents and conspicuous consumption. By the same token, the labor-market behavior of Brazil's native-born free population may also have stemmed from rational responses to economic conditions rather than from special cultural traits. Thus the Brazilians' often-cited preference for leisure, and the prevalence of 'vagabonds' and of other voluntarily underemployed people during the nineteenth century may have reflected labor-market demand and opportunity-cost conditions.[31] Such a pattern has in fact been observed in other pre-industrial societies, including some with decidedly non-Iberian or non-tropical cultures.[32]

The failure of Brazilian producers to adopt technological innovations from abroad sooner and on a wider scale has also been ascribed to the country's values. Again, the role of cultural rigidities in this process appears to have been exaggerated. For example, as early as 1813, Brazilians utilized a steam engine in sugar production; and in 1819, a steamboat was in operation on the Bay of Bahia.[33] Because of structural economic conditions, however, returns did not always justify widespread use of the new techniques in Brazil. David Denslow's detailed study of the Northeast sugar industry in the nineteenth century presents valuable information on this question. He concluded that in view of the factor and product prices which they faced, Northeast producers were fully rational in not shifting earlier from water to steam power, or from open kettles to vacuum pans.[34]

Similarly, considerable attention has often been directed to the relation between sociocultural conditions and entrepreneurship as a problem for economic development.[35] It seems unlikely, however, that Brazilian social structure or culture greatly inhibited the supply of entrepreneurship, and in that way slowed the country's economic development. Direct evidence on the connections between sociocultural conditions and the supply of entrepreneurship in nineteenth-century Brazil is not available. But the data noted earlier on the emergence and growth of new export commodities (rubber, erva maté, cacao, and coffee) attest to a strong willingness to adopt new crops and to open new lands to cultivation. The impression of vigorous expansionism which the figures convey is also corroborated by contemporary qualitative materials. Moreover, the qualities which permitted this activism and freedom from traditionalist rigidities were not confined to the often-cited entrepreneurs of São Paulo – rubber was produced in the Amazon region, and cacao in Bahia.

The Brazilian landowners' active quest for new sources of income and wealth should not be surprising. The aristocratic roots of much of the country's economic elite did not go deep at the beginning of the century. Notwithstanding its pretensions, this was a society in which wealth was the principal avenue to status.[36] Moreover, although Brazil's official culture was influenced by aristocratic currents, most Brazilian planters seem to have been people who were closer to the soil – and perhaps to the frontier – than to the imperial court at Rio de Janeiro. The fact that Brazil's economic elite also displayed non-economic behavior, such as conspicuous consumption, hardly controverts the presence of vigorous entrepreneurs. North American robber barons, too, often paraded their conspicuous consumption – to a degree that they helped provide the background for Thorstein Veblen's *Theory of The Leisure Class*.[37] Nevertheless, they were also noted for their entrepreneurship and their role in structural economic change. As the North American example indicates, entrepreneurship can coexist with social and cultural forms that may appear the antithesis of economic and developmental values. In fact, entrepreneurs from Brazil's landowner milieu played an important part not only in the country's agricultural expansion but in its industrialization as well.[38]

More generally, structural economic conditions in nineteenth-century Brazil seem to have been at the heart of some situations which have often been explained primarily in terms of social or cultural conditions. For example, the Northeast's poor experience during the nineteenth century has sometimes been attributed to non-adaptive behavior caused by the region's traditionalist values and social rigidities.[39] However, as we saw in Chapter 2, the region's problems were due mainly to macrostructural conditions. In such a context, even highly adaptive behavior at the microeconomic level can be of little avail.[40] Finally, the conditions under which sustained economic development began in nineteenth-century Brazil also provide a useful perspective on this general issue. The country's movement to accelerated economic progress seems to have followed directly from shifts in structural economic conditions.[41] And there is no indication that those shifts were preceded either by major changes in Brazilian social structure or by a psychocultural transformation of key segments in Brazilian society.

Further Discussion

The point of the preceding discussion is not that nineteenth-century Brazil was the best of all microeconomic worlds. Different social or cultural conditions might conceivably have permitted the country's economic development to begin earlier and proceed more satis-factorily. I am suggesting only that the problems which sociocultural conditions posed in Brazil have in some instances been exaggerated. And in other cases, it would be helpful to specify more clearly just how sociocultural conditions impeded the country's development, instead of treating institutional conditions as a catch-all explanation of the country's economic backwardness. Some illustrations may be useful here, and we can begin with the case of entrepreneurship.

Nineteenth-century Brazil may have had an ample supply of entrepreneurs who were willing and able to expand into new products and lands, but the alacrity with which new crops were taken up hardly resolved the country's development problems. Optimizing factor reallocation and extensive growth with existing techniques are not to be underrated. But they may have less impact on the growth of productivity and economic development than the capacity to *shift* production functions with the introduction of new techniques. Insufficient technological entrepreneurship seems to have shown itself in two ways in nineteenth-century Brazil. First, even taking account of such conditions as rates of return and capital-market imperfections, some techniques developed abroad *were* profitable to apply in Brazil. Nevertheless, the pace of adoption lagged. Inadequate technological entrepreneurship may well have been an important cause of such inertia. Second, a lack of technical entrepreneurship is indicated by the meager efforts of Brazilians to develop more productive technology which would have been suited to local ecological and economic con-ditions. In addition to raising productivity directly, such innovations might have increased the marginal productivity of capital and stimulated accelerated rates of capital formation.

Sociocultural conditions may well have been at the root of Brazil's limited technological entrepreneurship. However, this case also illustrates some of the difficulties which plague efforts at specifying the place of sociocultural conditions in the country's economic experience. Part of the cause of Brazil's modest rate of technical progress lay not in the paucity of innovations, but in the slow pace with which new technical information that *was* available spread through the economy. Thus, there are reports of individual planters developing more productive strains or productive techniques.[42] Brazilian intellectuals also provided relevant technical information. For example, early in the nineteenth century, a ten-volume encyclopedia was published in Brazil which made available to local planters translations of the best French and English works on tropical agriculture and on a wide range of other technological subjects.[43] Similarly, focusing on conditions in the local environment, Brazil's academies published monographs on the country's natural history, minerals, and agriculture.[44] However, this information seems to have diffused through the country relatively slowly.

The problem in the present context is to disentangle the impact of sociocultural conditions from that of other factors which also operated. Negative Brazilian values toward the acceptance of new techniques ('*rotinismo*') may clearly have slowed the pace of diffusion. But other conditions are pertinent too. For example, Brazil's low population densities and poor internal transportation conditions raised the costs of diffusing new information. In addition, the low educational levels which characterized nineteenth-century Brazil also retarded the spread of innovations. The widespread inability to read and write certainly increased the costs of disseminating information. Illiteracy and ignorance (rather than culturally-determined attitudes) may also have reduced people's propensity to adopt new techniques.[45]

Sociocultural conditions may of course have been the underlying cause of the country's high illiteracy rates. Such an interpretation is very plausible, for social stratification and culturally-based values affected both the demand and the supply of education. As attractive as this interpretation is, however, it may not be the whole story. For one thing, we must consider the question of how a large-scale expansion of education in nineteenth-century Brazil would have been financed. Undoubtedly, Brazilian governments would have had to mobilize much of the necessary resources. Unfortunately, the Brazilian state in the nineteenth century often faced serious public-finance constraints. In addition, during the first half of the century, the desire to maintain the country's political and territorial integrity was a more pressing priority for the state than was educational expansion.[46]

Further, another significant factor in Brazil's low literacy rates during much of the time span 1822–1913 derived not from the country's sociocultural conditions in the period under consideration, but from earlier history. Brazil began its post-independence period, in 1822, with very low enrollment ratios. As late as 1857 only about 1 percent of Brazil's population – approximately 7 percent of the relevant age cohort – was enrolled in the country's primary schools.[47] Thereafter, however, primary school enrollments seem to have expanded relatively rapidly. Between 1857 and 1889 the number of children enrolled in Brazil's primary schools increased at an annual geometric rate of approximately 3.7 percent. After 1889 primary school enrollments rose even faster, at an annual rate of some 5.1 percent between 1889 and 1907.

The causes of the acceleration of educational expansion in Brazil are not evident. It is not clear that the shift was sparked by major changes in the country's social structure or cultural conditions. And despite the increase in the number of literate people, Brazil's low educational level at the beginning of the century meant that the country's stock of human capital was to remain small for decades to come. The relevant variable from the viewpoint of technological innovation and diffusion is of course the stock (rather than the flow) of human capital. But, as just noted, Brazil's small stock of human capital during the nineteenth century owed much to a poor initial state rather than to the socio-cultural conditions which characterized the country during most of this period.

This discussion suggests a number of conclusions. We began by noting several instances where sociocultural conditions do not seem to have been a major obstacle to economic development in nineteenth-century Brazil. But it is also clear that a thorough analysis must go further, to identify and analyze cases where social structure and cultural conditions did pose serious problems. Unfortunately, it is not always simple to specify the role of sociocultural conditions *per se*, and to separate the effects of other factors. Partly because of these conceptual difficulties we are often left with an inconclusive (and therefore inherently unsatisfying) picture. Thus, present knowledge is often insufficient to permit more than conjectures in some important instances where social and cultural conditions may, in fact, have impeded Brazilian development.

A further example may help in elucidating these issues. This case involves another key area where sociocultural conditions may well have slowed down Brazil's economic development: the formation (and maintenance) of formal and informal associations for 'public improvements' such as capital formation and technical progress at the local level. Such voluntary groups for mutually beneficial ends can play an important role in providing public goods and external economies which are vital for the development process.[48] Cooperative activity along these lines was in fact important in development experiences which were otherwise very different, for example, in the United States and Japan.[49] Such associations for public improvements at the local and provincial levels seem to have been relatively absent, however, in nineteenth-century Brazil.[50] Special cultural values and/or social structure, for example, kinship patterns, may well have been responsible for this phenomenon.

This case also illustrates the same potential pitfall which we noted earlier: the propensity to focus mainly on sociocultural factors in explaining institutional features of nineteenth-century Brazil. Following that line of analysis, it would be easy to attribute the relative absence of local associations to Brazilian values – for example, a lack of the 'spirit of association' which Tocqueville found so important in the United States during the nineteenth century. But such a conclusion appears overly facile once we take a further view of the subject. Thus, some voluntary associations did flourish in nineteenth-century Brazil. These were the 'Commercial Associations', or interest groups, which operated mainly to further the fortunes of the country's urban merchants.[51] By contrast, four of the five agricultural associations which were founded (under government leadership) in 1860 disintegrated.[52] Again, it would be tempting to explain this disparate experience mainly in terms of differences between rural and urban values. Once more, however, other economic and political conditions must be included in the discussion. Thus, communications costs were much lower in Brazil's cities than in the rural areas. These differences presumably affected the net returns of establishing and operating voluntary associations in the two locales. Moreover, property relations must also be considered. The structure of land ownership in Brazil often involved the dominance of a few very large landowners within individual localities. Such a pattern may not have provided positive incentives for local cooperation. On the contrary, the stage may sometimes have been set for interclan rivalry, which did not promote increased supply of public goods. Furthermore, because of broader economic conditions, the operations of some local associations may have had a low economic return. Consistent with this last hypothesis is the fact that associations were founded in the Northeast, but languished. By contrast, groups that were established in São Paulo were strikingly successful in promoting European immigration and some local railways.[53]

The experience of Minas Gerais with respect to voluntary associations provides further support for an approach that includes economic conditions in the analysis. Prior to the 1890s, this large province had been noticeably lacking in such organizations. In the subsequent decade, however, the province experienced a sharp upsurge in associational activity.[54] The fact that this upsurge followed directly after the spread of railway construction in Minas Gerais may be more than coincidental. By lowering transportation costs, the railroads reduced the costs of organizing and maintaining province-wide associations. And by increasing the feasible scale of operations, the railways raised the returns which entrepreneurs and other individuals obtained from establishing and joining such associations. Thus the 'spirit of association' may have been present in Minas Gerais throughout the period; but before the expansion of the railroads, structural conditions had led to relatively low returns for such activities.

As in our earlier discussion of technological entrepreneurship and education, the point in the present context is primarily methodological. That is, we are not focusing here on choosing between alternative interpretations of an institutional feature which seems to have been important in Brazil's poor economic experience. (Indeed, the different explanations of these phenomena may often be complements rather than substitutes.) Rather, the purpose is simply to illustrate some of the complexities which must be considered before we can accept an interpretation which is based largely on sociocultural conditions.

Sociocultural Conditions and Brazil's Economic Historiography

Carried to an extreme, the proclivity to focus on sociocultural conditions can become a serious obstacle to the economic historiography of nineteenth-century Brazil. We have already noted a number of such possible distortions, and we can now draw together the discussion on this issue. One potential problem has been a tendency to view non-developmental behavior as stemming mainly from social and cultural factors. As we have seen, however, some important instances of economic 'deficiencies' in nineteenth-century Brazil can be explained largely by reference to economic conditions such as rates of return. Some additional examples help illustrate this phenomenon.

The planters in Brazil's export activities generally used slaves rather than indigenous free workers during the first half of the nineteenth century. This practice has often been attributed to planter preferences for maintaining master–slave hierarchical relations.[55] Brazil's planters may well have held such attitudes. But the fact that slave labor offered them higher profits is certainly also pertinent. In support of such an 'economic' interpretation, consider the Northeast's experience in this regard. Similar cultural attitudes are said to have prevailed in that region. However, the option of European immigration was not economically feasible in the Northeast; and the planters there made a smooth transition to the use of indigenous free workers. Likewise, the coffee planters of São Paulo have sometimes been cited for their modernizing attitudes in shifting, during the 1880s, from a labor system that depended on slaves to one that relied on European immigrant labor. This interpretation, however, neglects the *Paulistas'* earlier efforts to preserve a slave-based labor system by importing slaves from the Northeast. São Paulo's shift to immigrant labor came only after changes in labor-market conditions had made it economically rational to employ free workers.

The propensity to reach for explanations which are based primarily on sociocultural conditions has also led to other misperceptions. For example, nineteenth-century Brazil has sometimes been portrayed as a society that was structured in two classes, the masters and the slaves.[56] In fact, however, a large fraction of the country's population consisted of people who were neither masters nor slaves.[57] Thus, the 1872 census showed that even in the heart of the coffee region, fully 49 percent of the population was free, and only a fraction of these people were plantation owners.[58] The presence of an intermediate social stratum was even more marked in other parts of the country.[59] In addition, the nineteenth century saw a sharp rise in the number and percentage of free mulattoes, who came to constitute a lower-middle stratum in the country's social and economic structure.[60] The widespread acceptance of the earlier (and misleading) picture of nineteenth-century Brazil as a rigid, master–slave society is hard to understand. However, that picture may have been attractive because of the interpretive bias noted above. The existence of a two-class social structure would help provide an explanation, phrased in congenial sociocultural terms, for the country's poor economic experience during the nineteenth century.

We have also noted numerous instances in which purely economic conditions shed light on phenomena which have sometimes been discussed largely in terms of social institutions and cultural norms. Another example is the debate among historians concerning the degree of 'benevolence' of slavery in Brazil as compared with the United States or other slave-holding countries.[61] The relative frequency of manumission in Brazil has sometimes been construed as indicating a comparatively humane slave system. By contrast, over-working and high mortality rates for slaves suggest cruelty in Brazilian values. These seemingly contradictory phenomena pose an obvious problem for an interpretation that is framed primarily in cultural terms. They are easily resolved, however, in the context of an economic model of slavery in nineteenth-century Brazil.[62] Application of a high discount rate to the future income generated by slaves would lead to both of the phenomena observed: relatively high manumission rates for some young slaves, and overworking and high mortality for adults.

Finally, we have also seen that an excessive emphasis on social and cultural conditions in interpreting Brazil's history can lead to neglect of other relevant conditions. Such an approach has also affected some perceptions of Brazil's political history. For example, the country's success in avoiding the violence and instability which afflicted the Spanish-American countries after they achieved political independence has often been attributed largely to special characteristics of Brazilian personality and culture. As we will see in Chapter 5, however, certain structural features of the manner in which independence came in Brazil are crucial for explaining this pattern. Similarly, the tastes and personality traits which European immigrants brought to Brazil have sometimes been credited with a major role in the country's industrialization. But without some important economic shifts, for example, the emergence of an internal market based on coffee earnings and the expansion of the railways, the country's industrial development could not have been launched.[63] These shifts, moreover, did not depend on the arrival of European immigrants to Brazil. Hence the sociocultural changes which may have occurred as a result of European immigration were hardly central in the onset of Brazilian industrialization. As these examples indicate, by diverting attention from structural economic factors, a perspective which focuses largely on sociocultural conditions may even be misleading.

The foregoing discussion should not be misconstrued as suggesting that Brazilian economic historiography go to the opposite extreme, and analyze the country's economic history with an exclusively economic approach, to the exclusion of institutional considerations. On the contrary, we noted above some important areas – the relative absence of technological entrepreneurship and of local associations – where social and cultural conditions may have been of great importance for Brazil's economic retardation. Similarly, Brazil's illiberal land policy, which reflected the country's political ethos and structure, was responsible for major differences in nineteenth-century Brazil's economic experience as compared with the United States. I am merely proposing two obvious cautions: that sociocultural conditions not be invoked as a factotum explanation for Brazil's economic underdevelopment; and that such conditions not be substituted for analysis of the country's economic and political structure in cases where the latter are also relevant.[64]

Conclusions

This chapter has presented econometric results which indicate the presence of price responsiveness among Brazil's export producers in diverse commodities and regions during the nineteenth century. We have also noted instances of behavior elsewhere in the economy (e.g. low savings rates) which have sometimes been attributed to socio-cultural rigidities, but which are, in fact, consistent with economic rationality in the face of prevailing structural conditions.[65] Although it is possible to understand many features of nineteenth-century Brazil's economic experience without recourse to sociocultural conditions, this does not mean that such conditions were unimportant in the country's economic underdevelopment. But like any hypothesis, the manner in which sociocultural factors operated to slow economic development must be specified and examined carefully before we can accept their explanatory power. And following that approach, we have seen that the role of sociocultural conditions in Brazil's economic experience during the nineteenth century appears to have been less powerful than might have been expected.

Some readers may find it reassuring to find evidence of economic rationality in a society and culture as far removed from the wellsprings of classic capitalism as was nineteenth-century Brazil. Aesthetically, there may be a certain pleasure in contemplating an underlying human rationality which transcends space and time. And methodologically, it may be comforting to find support for the use of analytical models which presuppose market-responsive behavior. From another perspective, however, evidence for the existence of rational economic behavior in nineteenth-century Brazil is disturbing. As we noted in the case of cruelty to slaves, such rationality is consistent with behavior which is profoundly reprehensible on other grounds. Moreover, the Brazilian experience shows clearly that microeconomic rationality need not lead to economic development. Macrorationality – a society's capacity to solve structural problems which transcend the reach of individual microeconomic agents – is also necessary.

It would be foolhardy to conclude that social and cultural conditions had no effects on the pace and direction of Brazil's economic development during the nineteenth century. Such effects may well have obtained, operating through channels which our discussion has not captured. The point is simply that, at present, sociocultural conditions do not seem to provide a general explanation of Brazil's slow economic development in the nineteenth century. In a broader perspective, this conclusion comes as no surprise. Brazil had an economic experience very different from the United States, and may also have had a different social structure and culture. But there is no necessary logical basis for seeing those institutional conditions as the source of the different economic experience. Similarly, the range of sociocultural patterns, which are consistent with economically rational and expansionary behavior, is much wider than may have been imagined in earlier studies based on Northwest Europe and the United States. Thus, some societies with values and social structure very different from those of the private and individualistic capitalism which characterized New England and Manchester in the nineteenth century have also achieved rapid economic development. Ironically, the economic experience of the United States' ante-bellum South, with its planter aristocracy, used to be cited in support for an interpretation of Latin America's economic underdevelopment primarily in institutional terms.[66] Subsequent research, however, has shown that notwithstanding the ante-bellum South's special ethos and institutions, the region's economic performance compared favorably with that of New England and other regions of the United States.[67]

Finally, our earlier discussion suggested that in the search for the causes of Brazil's slow economic development during the nineteenth century, we focus on conditions in the country's political and economic structure. In the next chapters, we turn to that task.

Appendix

The text of this chapter presents the results of supply-response equations which were estimated for five Brazilian export commodities in two time periods (see Table 3.1, above). This Appendix explains the derivation of the estimating equation which provided the parameter estimates shown in Table 3.1.[68]

The hypothesis tested is that producers of individual export commodities in Brazil determined their annual production levels of the ith product in function of the prices which they expected to prevail when product i was harvested.

Further, since factors of production had alternative uses, producers also took into account the prices which they expected for this alternative (jth) commodity. We assume a lag of one year between the time when resources were allocated and output was sold; hence, expectations concerning prices in year t had to be formulated in year t-1.

For the reasons discussed in the text, the dependent variable specified in the regressions is the annual deviation of each export quantum series from its logarithmic trend. This variable, $q_{i,t}$ was taken as a function of the logarithm of the commodity's expected price, log $p^e_{i,t}$, and of the logarithm of the expected price for the jth commodity, log $p^e_{j,t}$. The approach utilized in order to generate the (unobservable) expected price series followed the adaptive-expectations model advanced by Marc Nerlove and others.[69] Thus,

$$\ln p^e_{i,t} - \ln p^e_{i,t-1} = \lambda_i (\ln p_{i,t-1} - \ln p^e_{i,t-1}) \qquad 0 < \lambda < 1 \qquad \text{(A.1)}$$

That is, the rate of change in the expected price of output i in period t is proportional to the difference between the actual and the expected price in the previous period. (The derivation of the expected price series for the jth products is similar; we therefore limit the discussion here to the ith product.)

Equation (A.1) can also be written:

$$\ln p^e_{i,t} = (1 - \lambda_i) \ln p^e_{i,t-1} + \lambda_i \ln p_{i,t-1} \qquad \text{(A.2)}$$

Lagging this equation one period, we obtain

$$\ln p^e_{i,t-1} = (1 - \lambda_i) \ln p^e_{i,t-2} + \lambda_i \ln p_{i,t-2} \qquad \text{(A.3)}$$

Substituting equation (A.2) into (A.1), and using the same lagging procedure, we can express log $p^e_{i,t}$ as a function of log p^e_{t-r} and a summation of observable log $p_{i,t-1-k}$ terms, where k ranges from zero to $r-1$. Letting $r = s-1$, we have

$$\ln p^e_{i,t} = (1 - \lambda_i)^{s-1} \ln p^e_{i,t-s-1} + \lambda_i \sum_{k=0}^{s=2} (1 - \lambda_i)k \ln p_{i,t-1-k} \qquad \text{(A.4)}$$

This formulation offers the following advantage: for $s < t$, we have actual observations for all the elements which appear in the second term on the right-hand side of (A.4). However, for all $s > t$, we still have unobservable elements in both the first and the second terms of (A.4).

In order to deal with this problem, I have followed the procedure of assuming that the expected price in the first year of the series was equal to the actual price in that year. In itself, this assumption is probably less heroic (i.e. far from reality) than might first appear. In any case, as (A.4) indicates, the importance of this initial assumption diminishes as we move further into the sample; that is, as $s (< t)$ grows larger, the term $(1 - \lambda_i)^{s-1}$ approaches zero. Further, the larger is λ_i the faster $(1 - \lambda_i)^{s-1}$ approaches zero, and hence the more rapid is the decline in importance of our initial assumption for the p^e_i series.

Given the initial condition that $\ln p^e_{i,1822} = \ln p_{i,1822}$, equation (A.1) tells us that the entire series $\ln p^e_{i,t}$ can be generated recursively once values are selected for λ_i. These values were selected by searching over a grid of different magnitudes for λ_i and λ_j. The λ values chosen for each commodity were those in the equation which gave the lowest standard error of estimate. The search was conducted (both for λ_i and for λ_j) over the following grid: 0.1, 0.2, 0.4, 0.6, 0.8, and 1. Search over a finer grid would undoubtedly have improved the efficiency of estimation, but even as is, computational costs were high. The procedure followed involved a total of thirty-six possible combinations for λ_i and λ_j in each of our twenty basic regression equations.

The a_1 and a_2 parameters of equation (1) are essentially long-run elasticities. Evidence on short-term supply elasticities, however, would constitute a much more demanding (and economically more important) test for the presence of supply rigidities in the nineteenth-century Brazilian economy. For this reason, equation (1) was not estimated directly. That approach would have permitted computation of the short-term elasticities ($a_1\lambda_i$ and $a_2\lambda_j$); but since the λ values are predetermined, we would not be able to evaluate the statistical significance of the short-run supply elasticities.

The approach adopted was the following. Dividing equation (A.3) by λ_i, we obtain

$$\frac{\ln p_{i,t}^e}{\lambda_i} = (1 - \lambda_i)\frac{\ln p_{i,t-1}^e}{\lambda_i} + \ln p_{i,t-1} \qquad (A.5)$$

Using the procedure outlined above for the initial value in the expected price series and for the values of λ_i, a series for ($\ln p_{i,t}^e$)/λ_i was generated. The same procedure was applied for the jth commodity's expected price. Equation (1) was then rewritten in the form

$$q_{i,t} = a_0 + a_1 \lambda_i \frac{\ln p_{i,t}^e}{\lambda_i} + a_2 \lambda_j \frac{\ln p_{j,t}^e}{\lambda_j} + u_t \qquad (A.6)$$

This was the estimating equation used. It permits direct estimation of the short-run supply elasticities ($a_1\lambda_i$ and $a_2\lambda_j$) and of statistics for testing their significance.

The procedures described above were necessary because our hypothesis is that producers adjusted their factor allocations and output to changes in *expected* relative prices. Some readers, however, may feel dubious about the application of elaborate statistical techniques to the data available for nineteenth-century Brazil. Moreover, these techniques open possibilities for generating statistical artifacts, or for 'data mining'. One may therefore want to see the results obtained from estimating a model which is econometrically more simple even if economically less appropriate.

Such a model was formulated and estimated. It involved regressing annual observations of the export quantum of individual commodities against the logarithm of *actual* relative prices. Because of the presence of strong trends in the price and quantity series, the variables were expressed as first differences. And because the object is to focus on price responsiveness in the short term, a constant was not specified in these equations, for such a constant term would in this specification capture the influence of trend. Since Brazil's export commodities were agricultural products with a minimum one-year gestation lag, the price variables were lagged. In the absence of prior information on the appropriate length of the lag, both one- and two-year lags were specified. Writing Q_i for the annual export quantum of the ith commodity, p_{ij} for its price relative to the price of the commodity with which it competed for factor utilization, and u for the stochastic term, we can express this simplified model as

$$\Delta\ln Q_{i,t} = a_1 \Delta\ln p_{ij,t-1} + a_2 \Delta\ln p_{ij,t-2} + u_t \qquad (A.7)$$

This equation was estimated for the same products and time periods as the regression equations whose results were shown in the text of this chapter. The parameter estimates and summary statistics for this econometrically simpler supply-response model are presented in Table 3.3.

Table 3.3 *Parameter Estimates and Summary Statistics from Supply Response Equations for Five Annual Export Commodities*

Product	Period	$\Delta\ln Q_i = a_1 \Delta\ln p_{ij-1} + a_2 \Delta\ln p_{ij-2} + u$ (absolute values of t-ratios are in parentheses)		
		a_1	a_2	D.W.
Cotton	1823–73	−.02 (.09)	.36** (2.01)	2.23
	1874–1913	−.56 (1.28)	.16 (.38)	2.50
Leather	1823–73	−.16 (.53)	.79 *** (2.63)	2.45
	1874–1913	.36 *** (2.24)	−.16 (.98)	2.08
Rubber	1833–73	.30* (1.65)	.15 (.86)	1.22
	1874–1913	.02 (.21)	.23** (2.18)	2.43
Sugar	1823–73	.28 (.77)	−.21 (.57)	2.26
	1874–1913	.85** (1.98)	−.18 (.41)	2.09
Tobacco	1823–73	.71*** (2.64)	.26 (.98)	2.56
	1874–1913	.86*** (4.24)	−.21 (1.07)	2.69

Note: An asterisk denotes a coefficient significant above the .10 level (with 30 degrees of freedom, critical $t=1.210$); two asterisks denote a coefficient significant above the .05 level (critical $t=1.697$); and three asterisks denote a coefficient significant above the .025 level (critical $t=2.042$). The jth products specified are: for cotton, tobacco in the earlier period, and sugar for the later period; for leather, sugar in the earlier period, and cotton in the later one; for rubber, cotton in the earlier period, and sugar in the later one; for sugar, cotton in both periods; and for tobacco, sugar in the earlier period, and cotton in the later one.

Equation (A.7) is not derived from a rigorous model of producer behaviour (i.e. one in which supply adjusts to changes in *expected* rather than in actual relative prices). Specification error should therefore lead to a relatively poor statistical fit for this equation. Nevertheless, the results presented in Table 3.3 support the hypothesis that producers in nineteenth-century Brazil responded to changes in relative prices. In eight of the ten equations, the hypothesis could be accepted at the 90 percent confidence level for at least one of the parameter estimates; and in seven equations, at the 95 percent level or higher. (The 'exceptions' were the same as in Table 3.1, and presumably for the same reasons discussed in the text there.) Moreover, the magnitudes of the supply elasticities were in five cases relatively high – greater than 0.7. Thus, the results of this crude model confirm the picture of supply-responsive behaviour which we obtained with the techniques discussed in this appendix.

Notes

1   See, for example, Sanford A. Mosk: 'To explain the sharp contrast between the United States and Latin America with respect to material development and standards of living, we must look mainly to institutional conditions which were established early and which have shown a strong tendency to persist.' This is from his paper 'Latin America vs. The United States,' *American Economic Review* (May 1951), p. 367. See also Bert F. Hoselitz, 'Economic Growth in Latin America,' *Contributions to the First International Conference of Economic History* (Paris: Mouton, 1960); and Seymour Martin Lipset, 'Values, Education, and Entrepreneurship,' in S. M. Lipset and Aldo Solari (eds), *Elites in Latin America* (New York: Oxford University Press, 1963). Among the interpretations which have stressed the importance of sociocultural conditions in explaining Brazil's economic retardation are Gilberto Freyre's classic *The Masters and the Slaves* (New York: Knopf, rev. edn, 1956); and Vianna Moog, *Bandeirantes and Pioneers*, trans. by L. L. Barrett (New York: G. Braziller, 1964).

2   The references cited in n. 1 all date from the first two decades of the post-Second World War period. Subsequently, emphasis by academics on sociocultural conditions as a barrier to economic development in Latin America declined. Nevertheless, an analysis of sociocultural constraints on Brazil's economic development is pertinent for a number of reasons. First, it would be helpful to know whether the change in intellectual emphasis is empirically justified in this case. Such an inquiry is also necessary because academic fashions on what constitutes a plausible conceptual framework can shift again in the future: one generation's dead horse can become another generation's galloping stallion. Finally, and perhaps most importantly, I find the hypothesis that sociocultural conditions played a role in nineteenth-century Brazil's poor economic experience has a certain *a priori* plausibility which commends it to serious consideration.

3   See, for example, William Baumol, *Welfare Economics and The Theory of The State*, 2nd edn (Cambridge, Mass.: Harvard University Press, 1965).

4   See, for example, William O. Jones, 'Economic Man in Africa,' *Food Research Institute Studies*, vol. 1 (May 1960); Edwin H. Dean, *The Supply Response of African Farmers* (Amsterdam: North-Holland, 1966); and Jere R. Behrman, *Supply Response in Under-Developed Agriculture: A Case Study of Four Major Annual Crops in Thailand, 1937–1963* (Amsterdam: North-Holland, 1968), and the studies reported in Chapter 1.

5   These data are presented in Instituto Brasileira de Geografia e Estatística, *Anuário Estatístico, 1939/40* (Rio de Janeiro, 1941).

6   On the points which follow, see, for example, P. Rao and L. Miller, *Applied Econometrics* (Belmont, California: Wordsworth, 1972), pp. 179–84; and Nathaniel H. Leff, *Underdevelopment and Development in Brazil*, Vol. 1: *Economic Structure and Change 1822–1947* (London: Allen & Unwin, 1982), Chapter 1, pp. 4–5.

7   See, for example, M. R. Wickens and J. N. Greenfield, 'The Econometrics of Agricultural Supply: An Application to the World Coffee Market,' *The Review of Economics and Statistics*, vol. 55 (November 1973).

8   See, for example, Pierre Monbeig, *Pionniers et Planteurs de São Paulo* (Paris: Armand Colin, 1952), pp. 84–8; António Delfim Netto, 'Foundations for the Analysis of Brazilian Coffee Problems,' in Carlos Manuel Peláez (ed.) *Essays on Coffee and Economic Development* (Rio de Janeiro: Instituto Brasileiro do Café, 1973), pp. 46–63.

9   Rubber was included in the list because it was collected from wild trees in Brazil.

10 A regression model along the lines discussed here is presented in Franklin M. Fisher and Peter Temin, 'Regional Specialization and the Supply of Wheat in The United States, 1867–1914,' *The Review of Economics and Statistics*, vol. 52 (May 1970).

11 In fact, the importation of slaves from Africa (and later, of subsidized immigrants from Southern Europe) made the supply of labor to some of Brazil's export activities (and hence trend) an endogenous variable which was determined by production opportunities within individual crops. See Leff, *Economic Structure and Change*, op. cit., Chapter 4.

12 Marc Nerlove, *The Dynamics of Supply: Estimation of Farmers' Response to Price* (Baltimore: Johns Hopkins University Press, 1958). The estimation procedures used follow those suggested in J. Johnston, *Econometric Methods*, 2nd edn (New York: McGraw-Hill, 1972), pp. 313–16; and Phoebus J. Dhrymes, *Distributed Lags: Problems of Estimation and Formulation* (San Francisco: Holden-Day, 1971), pp. 140–2.

13 As mentioned in the text, dividing the observations at 1873 rather than at another year is to some extent arbitrary. However, three reasons are relevant in explaining this division: (1) The year 1873 marked the onset of a major depression in the world economy. (2) For Brazil, 1873 divides the overall time span into two periods, in the first of which conditions with respect to slavery, railway construction, and European immigration were very different. (3) Finally, 1873 is not too far from the mid-point of the years 1822–1913.

14 Because of the first-order autoregressive structure and the estimation procedures used, the small-sample distribution of the parameter estimates in (1) cannot be derived. The *t*-ratios shown are therefore not exact. They can, however, be used for approximate tests of the null hypothesis that the parameter estimates do not differ significantly from zero. See the discussion in Phoebus J. Dhrymes, *Introductory Econometrics* (New York: Springer-Verlag, 1978), pp. 120–5.

15 Some of these commodities were produced in more than one of Brazil's regions and sub-regions. This circumstance implies a complex pattern of interrelations between various commodities for marginal factor supplies, and hence considerable statistical 'noise' in the parameter estimates for the a_2 term. In choosing the appropriate *j*th product to specify for the relative-price term in each equation, I was guided by material in Roberto C. Simonsen, *História Econômica do Brasil*, 4th edn (São Paulo: Companhia Editora Nacional, 1962); the work of a geographer, Preston James, *Brazil* (New York, 1942); and conversations with Professor Kempton Wood, of Columbia University's Latin American Institute and Department of Geography. The *j*th products which were specified were: for cotton, tobacco in the first period and sugar in the second; for sugar, cotton in both periods; for leather, cotton in both periods; for tobacco, sugar in the first period and cotton in the second; for rubber, cotton in the first period and sugar in the second.

16 The existence of positive serial correlation in these equations with a detrended dependent variable is unexpected. An economic explanation of this phenomenon is presented in Leff, *Economic Structure and Change*, op. cit., Chapter 6.

17 Peter Temin, 'The Causes of Cotton Fluctuations in the 1830's,' *The Review of Economics and Statistics*, vol. 49 (November 1967).

18 Further information on this compositional shift is presented in Leff, *Economic Structure and Change*, op. cit., Chapter 5, Table 5.5.

19 See, for example, Staffan B. Linder, *Trade and Trade Policy for Development* (New York: Praeger, 1966), esp. pp. 144–5.

20 See pp. 106–7 in Leff, *Economic Structure and Change*, op. cit., Chapter 6.

21 Caio Prado, Jr, *The Colonial Background of Modern Brazil*, trans. by Suzette Macedo from *Formação do Brasil Contemporáneo*, 7th edn (São Paulo, 1963) (Berkeley and Los Angeles: University of California Press, 1967), pp. 75–6, 89, 328–9.

22 Slavery was no impediment to an economically rational allocation of resources. On the contrary, with prices and sales in the country's slave market adjusting in an ongoing manner to changes in the marginal value product of labor in different activities, slavery was a prototypical institution of capitalism for nineteenth-century Brazil.

23 Caio Prado, *Colonial Background*, op. cit., p. 400.

24 An econometric study of agriculture in another underdeveloped and Catholic country in the nineteenth century, post-1850 Ireland, has also shown evidence of statistically significant supply response to prices. See Cormac O. Grada, 'Supply Responsiveness in Irish Agriculture during the Nineteenth Century,' *Economic History Review*, vol. 23 (May 1975).

25 Indeed, one approach suggests that at low income levels, there will be *less* adherence to cultural traditions which involve non-economic behavior. This would follow if we consider adherence to these traditions a good which, if it entails non-optimizing behavior, has a positive price. Hence, assuming diminishing marginal utility of money, there would be less non-economic behavior in underdeveloped countries. See Julian Simon, 'The Effect of Economic Status and Traditional Culture Upon Economic Behavior: An Optimistic Comment,' *American Journal of Agricultural Economics*, vol. 50 (May 1968).

26 Donald McCloskey has presented a list of distinguished scholars cited as adhering to this view. See his 'Review' of Samuel Popkin's *The Rational Peasant* (Berkeley: University of California Press, 1979) in *The Journal of Political Economy* (August 1981), p. 837.

27 See Chapter 4, pp. 76–7, below. The discussion there also considers (and rejects) the possible role of special risks and of information costs in accounting for the relatively small volume of foreign investment in Brazil until the 1890s.

28 See Leff, *Economic Structure and Change*, op. cit., Chapter 6, pp. 113–14.

29 Katia M. de Queirós Mattoso, *Bahia: A Cidade do Salvador e Seu Mercado no Século XIX* (São Paulo: Hucitec, 1978), p. 254.

30 Pedro Carvalho de Mello, 'The Economics of Labor on Brazilian Coffee Plantations, 1850–1888,' (PhD dissertation, University of Chicago, 1977), pp. 168–78.

31 See pp. 49–52 in Leff, *Economic Structure and Change*, Chapter 4.

32 See, for example, D. C. Coleman, 'Labour in The English Economy of The Seventeenth Century,' *Economic History Review*, (December 1955), pp. 280–95.

33 Mircea Buescu, *Evolução Econômica do Brasil* (Rio de Janeiro: APEC, 1974), p. 113; E. Bradford Burns, 'The Intellectuals as Agents of Change and the Independence of Brazil, 1724–1822,' in A. J. R. Russell-Wood (ed.), *From Colony to Empire* (Baltimore: Johns Hopkins University Press, 1975), p. 214.

34 David Denslow, 'Sugar Production in Cuba and Northeast Brazil, 1850–1914,' (mimeo., Yale University, 1972), Chapter 3. Denslow's conclusion (ibid., p. 26) is that: 'From the documents, one gains the impression that if northeastern sugar planters were not profit maximizers it was because they used new machinery too quickly, given local conditions, perhaps because they gained utility in consumption from ownership of the latest equipment.' Further discussion of relevant economic conditions (e.g. the prevalence of slavery and of capital-market imperfections) which slowed the pace of technical progress in nineteenth-century Brazil, see Leff, *Economic Structure and Change*, op. cit., Chapter 7.

35 Judgments may vary on the extent to which the supply of entrepreneurship constrained Brazil's economic development. The view that lack of entrepreneurship helps explain the country's tardy economic development is cited in Thomas E. Skidmore, 'The Historiography of Brazil, 1889–1964, Part II,' *Hispanic American Historical Review*, vol. 56 (February 1976), p. 94.

36 See, for example, Alan K. Manchester 'The Rise of the Brazilian Aristocracy,' *Hispanic American Historical Review*, vol. 11 (February 1931); Stanley J. Stein, *Vassouras: A Brazilian Coffee County* (Cambridge, Mass.: Harvard University Press, 1957), pp. 119–22; Monbeig, *Pionniers*, op. cit., pp. 84–5; and later in the century, on a province often considered to be highly traditionalist in its values, John Wirth, *Minas Gerais in The Brazilian Federation, 1889–1937* (Stanford: Stanford University Press, 1977), p. 73.

37 Max Lerner (ed.) *The Portable Veblen* (1899) (New York: The Viking Press, 1958), pp. 6–7. Similarly, for an earlier period in the United States, see Edward Pessen, *Riches, Class, and Power before the Civil War* (Lexington: D. C. Heath, 1973).

38 See Warren Dean, *The Industrialization of São Paulo, 1880–1945* (Austin: University of Texas Press, 1969), Chapter 3. Although much industrial entrepreneurship was supplied by local people in Brazil, a large share of the country's industrial entrepreneurship was supplied by immigrants. This may have been because of personality traits which made the immigrants (mainly from Italy and Portugal) better industrialists than native-born Brazilians. However, another interpretation suggests that personality or cultural differences *per se* may not have been important in determining the disparity. As relatively new arrivals to Brazil, immigrants were marginal to the broader society, and hence were less constrained by social pressures which may have inhibited local people from innovation and industrial entrepreneurship. Also, as newcomers, immigrants were more 'available', having fewer social ties that would constrain occupational mobility and thus raise the supply price of their entrepreneurship. Finally, immigrants often had important situational advantages. Because of their prominent role in peddling and retailing activities in Brazil, immigrants sometimes possessed superior information about local market conditions. Hence informational (and credit) advantages may have facilitated their entry to industrial entrepreneurship.

39 This interpretation in terms of sociocultural conditions has often been emphasized by a regional contrast. The alleged non-adaptive behavior of the planters in the Northeast has been contrasted with that of the São Paulo coffee *fazendeiros*, who are asserted to have had a more 'progressive' mentality.

40 It may be suggested that, in the final analysis, the Northeast's failure to find a higher-return alternative to sugar reflects the region's cultural rigidities. Charles P. Kindleberger has epitomized such institutionally-grounded rigidities in his emphasis on the importance of a society's 'capacity for transformation' for economic development. See his *Economic Development* (New York: McGraw-Hill, 1965), Chapter 10. However, the Northeast's experience with advisers from the Brazilian Southeast and from foreign countries like the United States in the twentieth century provides an enlightening perspective here. Those advisers have been free of the Northeast's special cultural traits. Nevertheless, they too have not been able to offer the Northeast much useful advice other than (non-feasible) structural changes or to recommend a massive infusion of external resources. These are solutions which Northeasterners themselves perceived (and frequently called for) during the nineteenth century.

41 See pp. 144–53 in Leff, *Economic Structure and Change*, op. cit., Chapter 7.

42 See, for example, Peter Eisenberg, *The Sugar Industry of Pernambuco: Modernization Without Change, 1840–1910* (Berkeley: University of California Press, 1974), pp. 33–4.

43 The work to which I refer is José Mariano da Conceição Veloso's *O Fazendeiro do Brazil*, as discussed in Charles R. Boxer, 'Historiography of Colonial Brazil, 1950–1970,' in Dauril Alden (ed.), *Colonial Roots of Modern Brazil* (Berkeley and Los Angeles: University of California Press, 1973), p. 14.

44 E. Bradford Burns, 'The Intellectuals as Agents of Change,' op. cit., pp. 218–9, 231–8. This study of the Brazilian academies at the turn of the eighteenth century reveals an intelligentsia that was oriented toward indigenous rather than to European concerns, and was empirical rather than *a prioristic* in its approach. This picture may clash with some standard views of the Brazilian intelligentsia during the nineteenth century. One possible explanation is that after the achievement of political independence, the focus of the country's intellectuals shifted away from domestic concerns.

45 Theodore W. Schultz, 'The Value of the Ability to Deal with Disequilibria,' *Journal of Economic Literature*, vol. 13 (September 1975).

46 On both points, see pp. 105–9 in Chapter 5, below.

47 These figures, and those presented later in this paragraph, were computed from data which are presented in Robert Havighurst and J. Roberto Moreira, *Society and Education in Brazil* (Pittsburgh: University of Pittsburg Press, 1965), p. 85. See also the discussion in Leff, *Economic Structure and Change*, op. cit., Chapter 2, pp. 18–20.

48 On the concept of public goods, see James M. Buchanan, *The Demand and Supply of Public Goods* (Chicago: Rand McNally, 1968); and Peter O. Steiner, 'Public Expenditure Budgeting,' in Alan Blinder *et al., The Economics of Public Finance* (Washington, D.C.: The Brookings Institution, 1974), pp. 243–58.

49 For an interesting case which illustrates the role of associations in reducing the transactions costs involved in technological diffusion, see Gary Saxonhouse, 'A Tale of Japanese Technological Diffusion in The Meiji Period,' *Journal of Economic History* (March 1974) esp. pp. 138–42, 160–1. Conversely, on the absence of local associations as an important explanation of a case of failure in economic development, see Edwin Banfield's analysis of Southern Italy, *The Moral Basis of a Backward Society* (Glencoe, Ill.: The Free Press, 1958). See also Albert O. Hirschman, *The Strategy of Economic Development* (New Haven: Yale University Press, 1958), pp. 11–19.

50 Cf. Richard Morse's comment: 'The *fazendeiro* . . . . had little capacity to unite with his peers in pursuit of broad common objectives.' This statement is from p. 175 of his essay 'Brazil's Urban Development,' in Russell-Wood (ed.), *From Colony to Empire*, op. cit. Similarly, Robert H. Mattoon, Jr has written of 'the extreme parochialism which . . . had blocked collective action' in providing São Paulo with railways. See his paper 'Railroads, Coffee, and the Growth in Big Business in São Paulo, Brazil,' *Hispanic American Historical Review*, vol. 57, no. 2 (May 1977), p. 285. Caio Prado's observations on the weakness of social organization in nineteenth-century Brazil may also be pertinent here. See, for example, his *Colonial Background*, op. cit., p. 403.

51 Eugene W. Ridings, 'Class Sector Unity in an Export Economy: The Case of Nineteenth-Century Brazil,' *Hispanic American Historical Review*, vol. 58 (September 1978). Ridings makes it clear that these associations operated in the country's major port cities, including Bahia and Maranhão, as well as Rio de Janeiro.

52 Ibid., p. 443.

53 Monbeig, *Pionniers*, op. cit., pp. 86, 92.

54 Wirth, *Minas Gerais*, op. cit., pp. 82, 58, 192–3.

55 See, for example, Warren Dean, *Rio Claro: A Brazilian Plantation System, 1820–1920* (Stanford: Stanford University Press, 1976), p. 123. The discussion in these two paragraphs draws on materials which are presented in *Economic Structure*, pp. 48–57. However, the focus here is on the methodological implications of that material for interpreting Brazil's economic past rather than on the substantive questions of labor-market supply and demand.

56 For an influential statement of this view, see Gilbert O. Freyre's *The Masters and The Slaves*.

57 Thus Caio Prado (*Colonial Background*, op. cit., p. 339) has spoken of '. . . the other sector of the colony's economy, comprising the small-scale agriculturalists and the small holders. For the humble independent copyholders and the small-time sugar planters, tobacco growers, or cotton planters – and as we have seen, there were large numbers of these – and even for the farmers raising food crops on the outskirts of the great agricultural centers . . . .'.

58 Stanley J. Stein, *Vassouras*, op. cit., p. 117.

59 For example, on the Northeast at the beginning of the period, see Stuart B. Schwartz, 'Elite Politics and the Growth of a Peasantry in Late Colonial Brazil,' in Russell-Wood (ed.), *From Colony to Nation*, op. cit., p. 134; and J. Riegelhaupt

and S. Forman, 'Bodo was Never Brazilian,' *Journal of Economic History*, vol. 30 (March 1970), esp. pp. 105–6. On the colonial period in Bahia see Stuart B. Schwartz, 'Free Labor in a Slave Economy: The Lavradores de Cana of Colonial Bahia,' in Alden (ed.), *Colonial Roots of Modern Brazil*, op. cit. Further information on these people (many of whom were in the domestic agricultural sectór) is presented in Leff, *Economic Structure and and Change*, op. cit., Chapter 2, pp. 20–22.

60   Herbert S. Klein, 'The Colored Freedmen in Brazilian Slave Society,' *Journal of Social History*, vol. 3 (March 1969).

61   An excellent survey of this debate is presented in John V. Lombardi, 'Comparative Slave Systems in the Americas,' in Richard Graham and Peter Smith (eds), *New Approaches to Latin American History* (Austin: University of Texas Press, 1974), esp. pp. 156–63.

62   See pp. 54–6 in Leff, *Economic Structure and Change*, op. cit., Chapter 4.

63   The discussion here is based on material which is presented in ibid., Chapter 7, pp. 144–9.

64   Other writers, including some with very different ideological perspectives, have come to the same conclusion. See, for example, André Gunder Frank, 'Capitalism and The Myth of Feudalism in Brazilian Agriculture,' in his *Capitalism and Underdevelopment in Latin America: Historical Studies of Chile and Brazil* (New York: Monthly Review Press, 1967), esp. p. 230. The similarity (in this respect) between Frank's emphasis on the 'capitalistic' nature of 'feudal' institutions in Brazil and the perspective of Theodore W. Schultz in his *Transforming Traditional Agriculture* (New Haven: Yale University Press, 1964) is clear.

65   Herbert Klein has pointed out to me the similarity between this general interpretation and that offered in a very different context by Witold Kula in his *An Economic Theory of The Feudal System: Toward a Model of The Polish Economy, 1500–1800* (1962) (New York: Schocken, 1976).

66   Mosk, 'Latin America vs. The United States,' op. cit., pp. 379–80.

67   Specifically, both the level of income and the rate of output growth per worker were as high in the ante-bellum South as in the rest of the United States. See Richard A. Easterlin, 'Interregional Differences in Per Capita Income, Population, and Total Income, 1840–1950,' in Conference on Research in Income and Wealth, *Trends in The American Economy in The Nineteenth Century* (Princeton University Press, 1960); and Robert Gallman, 'Gross National Product in The United States, 1834–1909,' Conference on Research in Income and *Wealth, Output, Employment, and Productivity in The United States after 1800* (New York: National Bureau of Economic Research, 1966). One can of course always ask whether, with a different social structure and culture, the South might not have enjoyed an even more rapid pace of development. Within a holistic view of society and economy, the meaning of that question is not completely clear. In any case, the South's actual historical record is sufficient for the purpose of the present discussion.

68   John Millar made valuable suggestions concerning the econometric formulations discussed below.

69   See n. 12, above.

4

Imperialism

This chapter considers some effects which economic and political forces external to Brazil may have had in delaying or distorting the country's economic development. We will discuss both the direct impact of Brazil's increasing integration in the world economy, and the effects which may have followed from loss of domestic control over key decisions affecting the national economy. The subject of imperialism is obviously connected with broader ideological issues. Perhaps because of this reason, scholars with differing perspectives have not always found dialogue in this area easy.[1] However, by focusing on some specific issues in Brazil's historical experience, we may achieve some analytical progress at least in this particular case.

Some Direct Effects of Imperialism

Brazil was not formally a colony during the nineteenth century. However, it has been suggested that the country was part of the 'informal' British empire, and that the economic and political relations which this connection entailed slowed or distorted Brazil's development.[2] Great Britain did have considerable diplomatic influence in Brazil, especially in the first half of the century. Moreover, in the period from 1810 to 1844 a treaty imposed by the British limited Brazil's import duties to 15 percent *ad valorem*. Brazil's inability to levy truly protective import tariffs before 1844 may well have delayed the country's first movement toward industrialization.

With the expiration of the treaty, the Brazilian government raised the country's tariffs.[3] The tariffs were levied in accordance with procedures which varied over time. In particular, the alternation of specific and of *ad valorem* rates makes it difficult to compute the exact height of the tariff. One fact, however, is clear. The imposition of higher import duties raised the cost of imported goods in Brazil appreciably. Table 4.1 presents information on this price effect. In addition, the Brazilian government also levied taxes on the country's exports. These taxes, too, altered relative prices in a manner which raised the returns to potential import-competing activities such as manufacturing.[4] Column (3) of Table 4 shows the magnitude of import duties and export taxes as a percentage of the value of Brazil's

Table 4.1   *Import and Export Taxes as a Percentage of the Value of Brazilian Imports, 1831–1885*

(1) Period	(2) Import Duties as a Percentage of The Value of Imports	(3) Import and Export Duties as a Percentage of The Value of Imports
1831–40	15	20
1841–50	24	30
1851–60	26	29
1861–70	27	36
1871–80	36	47
1881–85	39	48

Source: Computed from data in Marcio Teixeira, 'Public Finance in the Brazilian Empire,' (mimeo., Columbia University, New York, 1970), Table 8 and Appendix Table 2.

imports between 1831 and 1885. Potential infant industrialists in Brazil were of course also protected by the high international transportation costs which prevailed in the pre-steamship era.

Industrial output, particularly of cotton textiles, expanded rapidly following the tariff increases.[5] However, a large-scale industrialization process, in which manufacturing output would have accounted for a sizable share of Brazil's GNP, needed more than protection against imports.[6] As discussed below, the country's industrial development required the emergence of a domestic market for manufactures. When domestic income and the demand for industrial products did expand, the Brazilian government provided protection, and the country's industrial development proceeded apace, regardless of the preferences of foreign imperialist powers.[7]

Declining international terms of trade have also been proposed as a mechanism by which imperialist powers might impoverish weaker countries. In fact, however, Brazil's income and barter terms of trade did not deteriorate during the nineteenth century. Brazil's export-price index showed an upward trend. At the same time, world prices for manufactured products, Brazil's chief import good, declined steadily. Thus, both on the import and on the export sides, Brazil's terms of trade generally improved rather than worsened during the nineteenth century.[8]

Foreign-capital payments were another channel by which international economic relations might in principle have transferred income from Brazil and kept the country poor. Measures of the total volume of Brazil's overseas payments on capital account during the nineteenth century are not available. However, some partial evidence suggests that the magnitudes of the country's foreign-capital payments were not large enough to impoverish a country the size of Brazil. One possible indicator of the overseas drain is the extent to which foreign-

Table 4.2 *The Value of Brazilian Commodity Imports as a Percentage of the Value of The Country's Commodity Exports, 1821–1910*

Period	IMP/X		Period	IMP/X
1821–30	1.09		1871–80	.83
1831–40	1.11		1881–90	.88
1841–50	1.12		1891–1900	.88
1851–60	1.11		1901–10	.70
1861–70	.89			

Note: The *IMP* figures understate the value of Brazilian imports before 1852 because they do not include the country's substantial importation of slaves from Africa.

Source: Computed from annual data on the value of imports and exports available in Instituto Brasileiro de Geografia e Estatística, *Anuário Estatístico do Brasil, 1939/1940*, vol. 5, pp. 1358–9.

capital payments diminished the value of commodity imports relative to the country's export receipts. This measure is, of course, the country's balance of trade, the ratio of the country's imports (IMP) to its exports (X). Table 4.2 presents decadal figures for the balance-of-trade ratio in nineteenth-century Brazil. A ratio less than unity ($IMP/X < 1$) might indicate a drain on Brazilian resources via the external sector.

Table 4.2 shows that in the first half of the century, the value of Brazil's commodity imports exceeded the value of the country's exports. Presumably this phenomenon reflects the existence of positive foreign-capital inflow. Thereafter, the IMP/X ratio fell below unity, as uses other than commodity imports took an increasing share of the country's export receipts. This reversal should not be surprising, however; the foreign capital which had earlier permitted an excess of imports over exports had to be serviced. Moreover, the decline in commodity imports relative to exports also stemmed from a cause other than foreign-capital payments, namely, overseas remittances on the part of Brazil's growing immigrant population. Thus the IMP/X ratio fell sharply in the years 1901–10. Remittances by Italian immigrants to Brazil increased markedly during that period.[9]

Another qualifying consideration must also be mentioned. Our discussion thus far has accepted the assumption that the welfare effects of a balance-of-trade ratio less than unity ($IMP/X < 1$) were unambiguously negative for Brazil. That assumption can be questioned, however. To some extent, foreign investment in Brazil contributed to an expansion of the country's exports. This was especially the case in the last decades of the century, when much of Brazil's foreign loans and investment went to enlarge infrastructure in the economy's export sector. Thus foreign capital inflow helped generate an increase in X as well as an increase in capital-service payments (and a balance-of-trade ratio less than unity). Under such conditions, an 'adverse' ratio of IMP

to X might be associated with higher levels of Brazilian exports and income.

More generally, the magnitude of international transfers does not seem to have been substantial relative to the size of the Brazilian economy. The channel through which Brazilian income were transferred overseas was the country's export sector. However, export production did not constitute a very large share of aggregate income in Brazil during the nineteenth century.[10] Further, Table 4.2 shows that the most significant use of export income was commodity imports rather than overseas transfers.

The issue of foreign capital also raises the question of whether the interest and profits on foreign loans and investments in Brazil were in some sense excessive. A definitive answer to that question would require an analysis of the returns which foreign investors obtained in Brazil relative to the opportunity cost of foreign capital. The latter would reflect the returns which foreign capitalists could have obtained in their best alternative investments with similar economic characteristics (e.g. risk and uncertainty). Such an analysis would require a major study in itself. Fortunately, we can take a more direct approach to this question.

Great Britain was the single largest source of international investment during the nineteenth century. Hence, if the returns which foreign capitalists were able to extract from Brazil had been unusually high relative to the alternative uses of these investment resources (at home or abroad), one would expect to observe a relatively large flow of British investment to Brazil. The gains made possible by imperialism might be reflected either in a large absolute volume of capital flows, or in a relatively large share for Brazil in Great Britain's total international investment. In fact, as Table 4.3 indicates, the magnitudes of British investment to Brazil were not very great until the end of this period. Further, despite Brazil's relatively large size, the country did not receive a large percentage of either total British overseas investment or British investment in Latin America (see Table 4.4).

British investment in Brazil was not deterred by extraordinary risk conditions or by unusually high costs of obtaining information (see below). Hence, the relatively small share and magnitude of British investment until the last decade of the century suggest that the returns to British investment in Brazil were not especially attractive. A conclusion that imperialism did not permit foreign capitalists to appropriate unusually high profits in Brazil is also consistent with our earlier suggestion that international investment did not operate as a powerful 'suction pump' draining income from Brazil. Indeed it is not clear that one should expect a close connection between imperialism and generalized high returns to foreign investors in the nineteenth century. The largest single recipient of British capital exports during the period

Table 4.3 *Average Annual Flow of British Loans and Portfolio Investment in Brazil, 1865–1914*

Period	Annual Value in Current Prices (£m.)	Annual Value in Constant (1880) Prices (£m.)
1865–69	1.2	0.9
1870–74	1.1	0.9
1875–79	1.6	1.5
1880–84	2.8	2.9
1885–89	4.4	5.2
1890–94	1.0	1.2
1895–99	2.0	2.6
1900–04	1.1	1.3
1905–09	5.5	6.2
1910–14	13.4	14.4

Source: Computed from data presented in Irving Stone, 'The Annual Flow of British Capital to Latin America, 1865–1914,' paper presented to the Sixth International Congress on Economic History, Copenhagen, 1974, Table 5. The data show the actual payments made by foreign lenders and investors in acquiring new Brazilian floatations in Great Britain. To convey an idea of the value of this capital inflow to Brazil in constant prices, the British export price index was used as a deflator. This series is available in Albert H. Imlah, *Economic Elements in the Pax Britannica* (Cambridge, Mass.: Harvard University Press, 1958), pp. 94–8.

was the United States, an appendage of neither Britain's formal nor 'informal' empires.[11]

Toward the end of the nineteenth century, the United States replaced Great Britain as the power with preeminent diplomatic influence in Brazil. It is not apparent, however, how the United States' diplomatic position slowed Brazilian economic development. Brazil's exports to the United States entered the American market duty-free or nearly so, while the average Brazilian tariff on goods from the United

Table 4.4 *Brazil's Share in the Flow of New British Overseas Loans and Portfolio Investment to Latin America and to the World, 1865–1914*

Period	Brazil's Share of Total British Portfolio Investment in Latin America (%)	Brazil's Share of Total British Portfolio Investment (%)
1865–74	13	2
1875–84	38	5
1885–94	14	4
1895–1904	19	2
1905–14	25	6
1865–1914	21	4

Source: Computed from data in Irving Stone, 'The Annual Flow of British Capital to Latin America, 1865–1914,' paper presented to the Sixth International Congress on Economic History, Copenhagen, 1974, Tables 1 and 5. Note that Stone's data cited here refer to the actual payments made by foreign lenders and investors in acquiring new foreign floatations in Great Britain.

States was 45 percent.[12] United States pressure on Brazil to have these tariffs reduced met with only limited success due to the protectionism of the Brazilian Congress. Further, Brazil levied an export tax on coffee. Because of the price inelasticity of United States demand, this tax involved a transfer of income from American consumers to Brazilian producers. Consequently, in terms of optimum tariff theory, Brazil seems to have exploited the United States rather than vice versa. The size of this income transfer may not have been large; but the mere fact of its existence raises doubts concerning the view that United States imperialism was exploiting Brazil during this period.[13]

A Broader View of Imperialism and Its Distortions

Our discussion thus far has focused on relatively narrow phenomena – tariffs, Brazil's international terms of trade, and possible economic retardation through international capital flows. In a broader approach, some writers have criticized Brazil's entire pattern of economic expansion during the nineteenth century as colonial. Following this critique, the country's emphasis on exports and the relative neglect of industrialization was a distortion which reflected pressures emanating from the international economy.

As we saw elsewhere, the growth of Brazil's exports in the nineteenth century seems to have been the country's response to the expanding markets and favorable relative-price movements which the world economy offered at that time.[14] The income gains which derived from rising exports were of special value in an economy that was otherwise relatively stagnant in terms of total factor productivity increase. One may be tempted to dismiss the higher income which export growth generated as reflecting only static efficiency gains. However, criticism of nineteenth-century Brazilian growth for relying on exports also errs about the dynamic effects. The fact that Brazil's industrial development was concentrated in the same region (São Paulo and Rio de Janeiro) as the country's coffee production cautions against a hypothesis that primary-product exports retarded Brazilian industrialization. On the contrary, export expansion seems to have promoted domestic industrial development in this case.[15] Export growth was particularly important for enlarging the internal market for manufactured goods in Brazil. First, the higher income which came from coffee production generated increased demand for industrial products. In addition, the expansion of the railways which was associated with export growth lowered internal transportation costs within Brazil, and helped provide the domestic market for manufactures which was essential for the country's industrialization.

It may be suggested that if exports had not expanded in Brazil during the nineteenth century, the country would have embarked on another

– and perhaps healthier – development path. That would have been a pattern of autonomous development, based on activities oriented toward the local market. That alternative model, however, is premised on two crucial assumptions: that the economy achieves significant productivity gains in its domestic sector; and that it does so independently of export growth.[16] Those conditions were probably not satisfied in nineteenth-century Brazil. The country's low educational levels and poor transportation facilities were serious barriers here.[17] And it is hard to argue that if Brazil had had less contact with the international economy during the nineteenth century, the country's stock of social-overhead capital would have been in a better state. On the contrary, export growth was of central importance for the improvement of the country's economic infrastructure over the nineteenth century. Foreign investment in infrastructure projects was often closely connected with export opportunities. Similarly, the Brazilian government's tax revenues and its fiscal capacity to provide resources for developmental purposes (e.g. railway construction) were tightly linked to the growth of the country's foreign trade (see below).[18] Note further that some of the infrastructure facilities which Brazil's export sector generated also benefited activities in the domestic sector of the economy. For example, the decline in transportation costs which came with expansion of the railways in Brazil helped the domestic agricultural sector as well as the export producers. Indeed, the fall in internal freight costs seems to have been much greater for the bulky, low-value products of the domestic agricultural sector than for the higher-value export products.[19]

The experience of the Northeast suggests what might have happened to Brazil's development if the country's foreign trade had not expanded during the nineteenth century. Lacking buoyant exports, the Northeast did not start on a vigorous pattern of autonomous development. Instead, the region suffered from economic stagnation. To be sure, the Northeast's underdevelopment was aggravated by the exchange-rate effects which we analyzed in Chapter 2. But as the discussion there also indicated, the primary cause of the region's poor economic development during the nineteenth century was the failure to achieve higher export growth. Indeed, historians have rarely considered the possibility that the Northeast might have experienced sustained economic development based on the domestic sector. In view of the historical realities of the region's meager stock of social overhead capital, that 'alternative' has appeared too implausible to merit serious consideration.

The long delay before export growth led to a more generalized pattern of economic development in Brazil can be interpreted as indicating how useless was a process of export-led development. The opposite interpretation, however, may be more accurate. The fact that it took so long for widespread development to begin, despite the stimulus which expanding trade gave to monetization, infrastructure formation, and the other structural changes noted elsewhere,[20] shows how limited was the capacity of this economy for a pattern of autonomous development. These considerations suggest that because of the country's internal conditions, export-led development was probably the only development scenario that was realistically feasible for nineteenth-century Brazil. From this perspective, economic development was held back in nineteenth-century Brazil not because of the country's concentration on international trade, but because the country's exports did not expand sufficiently.

It may be proposed that export growth during the century ultimately hurt Brazil, by locking the country into economic and social patterns which retarded subsequent development in the twentieth century. Any such historical appraisal, however, should presumably utilize a positive discount rate. Such discounting is necessary to evaluate, from the viewpoint of the nineteenth century, putative income losses in the twentieth century. Discounting over such long time periods would greatly reduce the relevant present value of any such losses. Moreover, some factual (as opposed to counterfactual) considerations are also pertinent in this discussion. Even in undiscounted terms, it is not apparent that any losses were involved. In fact, nineteenth-century export expansion did *not* thwart twentieth-century industrial development in Brazil. When relative prices and expected returns changed, investment and production in the Brazilian economy adjusted successfully to a pattern in which domestic industrialization rather than exports led the country's development.[21]

Imperialism and Dependency

Imperialism may also entail the loss of domestic control over the policy decisions which affect a country's economic progress. Two issues are involved here. First, lack of autonomy leads to diminished dignity and self-esteem. Second, the decisions taken by foreigners may not be those which are best suited to the country's own economic interests.

At the beginning of the century, Brazil undoubtedly did lack full autonomy in making economic-policy decisions. For example, the 1810 treaty mentioned earlier limited Brazil's power to increase its import duties. Nevertheless, in a case where sizable Brazilian interests were involved, the country was able to resist substantial imperialist pressures. Thus, for almost half a century (!), Brazil was able to withstand Britain's pressures to stop the importation of slaves from Africa. This successful resistance occurred despite Britain's dominant position in Brazil's foreign trade and international borrowing. And when the British eventually used coercion to stop the traffic, relations were so embittered that Britain's diplomatic preeminence in Brazil declined sharply thereafter.[22]

The measures imposed on Brazil during the period of imperialist dominance were (presumably) beneficial to the British. It does not necessarily follow, however, that these decisions were also prejudicial to Brazilians. Thus, in 1808 Britain forced the opening of Brazil's ports to direct trade with countries other than Portugal. This shift eliminated the use of Portugal as an entrepôt for Brazil's imports and exports. It also permitted the entry of additional traders into what had earlier been monopoly positions. The elimination of transshipment charges and the increased market competition which these changes engendered probably raised the prices received by Brazil's exporters, and lowered the prices which Brazil paid for its imports. Consequently, it is likely that both Brazil and Britain benefited from the opening of the ports.[23]

Similarly, Britain's termination of the transatlantic slave traffic was a blatant trespass on Brazilian sovereignty. Nevertheless, the intrusion need not be considered completely bad in its effects, for it helped end the existence of slavery in Brazil.[24] Indeed, modernizing groups in Brazilian society favored abolition, as did the slaves themselves. As these cases indicate, the effects of imperialism on national dignity and on economic progress may work in opposite directions. As Marx emphasized, international capitalism was often a progressive force in its impact on underdeveloped countries during the nineteenth century.[25]

By the end of the century, foreign control over Brazilian decision-making had clearly diminished. Thus, in the 1890s the Brazilian government maintained a policy of monetary expansion despite overt opposition from the country's foreign bankers.[26] The government was also able to oblige the foreign railway companies to lower their rates on domestically-produced foodstuffs.[27] And when exchange depreciation raised the domestic-currency burden of capital-service payments to foreign railway companies, the Brazilian government nationalized some foreign holdings.[28] Finally, the pressures of foreign importing countries did not stop the Brazilians from proceeding with valorization programs to raise international coffee prices. Indeed, perhaps in recognition of their inability to veto the program, international bankers actually provided the finance that was used to implement it.[29]

Overall, then, imperialist control over Brazilian policy-making does not seem to have played a large role in Brazil's poor economic experience during the nineteenth century. Following a different line of reasoning, Celso Furtado reached a similar conclusion even for the *first* half of the century.[30] And in the second half of the period, Brazil had greatly increased its autonomy and capacity to withstand external influence. Objective economic conditions and internal pressures had now become the major determinants of the country's economic-policy decisions.[31]

Ideological Dependency

Brazil was also able to avoid another, more subtle, form of imperialist domination: excessive deference to economic doctrines and ideologies emanating from the metropolitan countries, but not necessarily appropriate for a country like Brazil.[32] Doctrines of *laissez-faire* and of gold-standard orthodoxy were frequently propounded in nineteenth-century Brazil. But metropolitan ideologies rarely dominated actual policy-making in Brazil. The country's political elite operated with a degree of ideological autonomy which enabled them to follow economic policies that were often markedly heterodox in practice.

Following their earlier experience with the inefficiencies of Portuguese mercantilism, Brazilian elites were initially wary of pervasive government intervention in the economy.[33] Moreover, *laissez-faire* policies were sometimes pursued because of domestic self-interest rather than an affinity for imported ideologies. Brazilian policy often departed from classical liberalism, however, if the interests of the state were involved or if market forces led to outcomes which policy-makers believed government action could ameliorate.[34] Thus, in 1841 direct subsidies were used to promote the establishment of some factories in Rio de Janeiro.[35] More generally, Brazilian governments in the nineteenth century intervened to subsidize a variety of activities: coastal steamboats, railway construction, modernization of sugar technology in the Northeast, and European immigration. Similarly, in the first decade of the twentieth century, the coffee valorization program mentioned earlier was another deviation from *laissez-faire*. In this the government intervened directly in the market to control Brazilian production and raise international coffee prices.[36]

In the area of macroeconomic policies, it was also uncommon for Brazilian policy-makers to be constrained by the economic doctrines propagated in the metropolitan countries.[37] In practice there were often departures from the canons of nineteenth-century orthodoxy. For example, in fiscal policy, far from keeping expenditure in balance with revenue (or perhaps maintaining a tidy surplus), Brazil's central government usually had its budget in deficit. Table 4.5 presents data on the frequency and magnitude of budget deficits between 1823 and 1888.[38] As the data indicate, balanced budgets were the exception rather than the norm. Moreover, budget deficits that were of more than negligible size were common. The government's expenditures exceeded its receipts by more than 15 percent in thirty-four of

Table 4.5 *Frequency and Magnitude of Central-Government Budget Deficits in Brazil, 1823–1889*

Number of Years	Government Deficits, D, as a Percentage of Government Revenues
3	$-20\% \leq D < -15\%$
4	$-15\% \leq D < -5\%$
4	$-5\% \leq D < 0$
13	$0 \leq D < 5\%$
8	$5\% \leq D < 15\%$
7	$15\% \leq D < 20\%$
15	$20\% \leq D < 50\%$
9	$50\% \leq D < 100\%$
3	$D > 100\%$

Source: Computed from data in Oliver Ónody, *A Inflação Brasileira* (Rio de Janeiro, 1960), pp. 197–9.

these sixty-six years; and by more than 50 percent, in twelve years.

Not only in fiscal policy but in monetary policy, too, the Brazilian authorities often deviated from the norms of metropolitan orthodoxy. Thus the international trade balance rarely influenced the pace of monetary expansion in Brazil during the nineteenth century.[39] Rather, internal considerations predominated in determining the growth of the country's monetary stock. And responding to domestic pressures, the Brazilian government did not let conventional doctrine deter it from expanding the money supply at a rate which led to secular inflation.[40] Not surprisingly, price inflation at a rate above world-market levels helped cause long-term depreciation in Brazil's exchange rate. This currency depreciation is especially noteworthy because it occurred despite favorable long-term movements in the country's terms of trade. Finally, the Brazilian authorities generally did not follow a gold-standard exchange-rate policy. Although there were occasional efforts to maintain the exchange rate at a fixed parity, these did not prevent the long-term depreciation just noted. Rather than deflate domestic income in order to defend the parity, the government usually permitted the exchange rate to depreciate.

As these examples from exchange-rate, monetary, and fiscal policy indicate, Brazilian policy-makers could (and did) act independently of the orthodoxies propounded in the metropolitan countries during the nineteenth century. Because of this ideological and political autonomy, Brazil was able to implement a set of economic policies very different from those of underdeveloped countries which were under imperialist control. We leave to the next chapter a discussion of the effects of these policies. The point in the present context is that foreign ideologies rarely constituted a rigidity which limited the opportunities that were available to Brazilian policy-makers.

The Limited Degree of Imperialist Control

A complete analysis of the conditions which permitted Brazil's doc-trinal and economic-policy autonomy is beyond the scope of the present study. But in view of the importance of the question, we note some relevant points.

To some degree, the macroeconomic policies we have discussed simply reflected the fiscal exigencies of the state. The economic and political conditions prevailing in Brazil during the nineteenth century placed sharp limitations on the tax revenues that were available to the Brazilian government.[41] In that context, deficitary public finance and inflationary rates of monetary expansion were often used to ease the constraint on government expenditure levels. Heterodox fiscal and monetary policies, in turn, would not have been feasible under a gold-standard exchange-rate policy. Although fiscal pressures clearly were important in accounting for Brazil's unconventional economic policies, such conditions in themselves do not provide a sufficient explanation. The country's policy-makers also had to have sufficient ideological autonomy to formulate economic policy pragmatically, relatively free of the shackles imposed by metropolitan ideologies. The intellectual and social conditions which permitted this degree of doc-trinal liberation in nineteenth-century Brazil require further study.

One aspect of this situation is clear, albeit paradoxical. In some ways, Brazil's capacity for autonomous policy action increased as a direct result of the country's involvement in the international economy. First, the Brazilian state grew directly as a function of the country's foreign trade. This was because taxes levied on international trans-actions provided the state with most of its fiscal resources in the nineteenth century. Table 4.6 provides information on this phenom-enon. As the data indicate, the external sector generated a large portion of the Brazilian government's total revenues. Further, as shown in the next chapter, the growth of the country's foreign trade led to a *pari passu* increase in government receipts and expenditures

Table 4.6   *The Share of Foreign-Trade Taxes in Total Revenues of Brazil's Central Government, 1831–1885*

Period	Percent	Period	Percent
1831–35	45	1861–65	76
1836–40	80	1866–70	73
1841–45	71	1871–75	71
1846–50	73	1876–80	68
1851–55	81	1881–85	69
1856–60	78		

Note: Foreign-trade taxes include import duties, export taxes, and marine duties.
Source: Computed from figures which are presented in Márcio Teixeira, 'Public Finance in the Brazilian Empire' (mimeo, Columbia University, 1970), Table 7.

between 1822 and 1913. These resources were of special significance for the development of the state as an institution because public finance was in any case relatively scarce in nineteenth-century Brazil.[42] And state-building was important in the present context, for the Brazilian government was the only institution which could possibly have acted as a counterpoise to domination by foreign interests.

In a similar dialectic, the external sector also helped promote the growth of the Brazilian intelligentsia. Because of its influence on monetization and the spread of markets, export expansion was an important factor in the growth of Brazil's cities. The urban sector, in turn, was crucial for the enlargement of the intelligentsia in nineteenth-century Brazil. Many of the intellectuals who were nationalistically-oriented (by nineteenth-century standards) had their social milieu and economic base in the urban sector or in the state apparatus.

The limited external control over Brazilian policy-making during the second half of the century was also facilitated by other conditions. In the course of this period, the country's foreign trade became increasingly diversified, both in terms of export markets and in terms of import supply. Thus Great Britain's predominant position in the supply of Brazil's imports was increasingly challenged by European countries and the United States.[43] Similarly, after 1860, Britain's share in Brazil's exports fell sharply. As Table 4.7 indicates, the United States became the largest single market for Brazil's overseas sales. At the same time, the share of North America in Brazil's exports of *coffee* – a commodity of special economic and political importance in Brazil – declined significantly. Between 1880 and 1900, North America's share in Brazil's overseas coffee sales fell from 58 to 39 percent; while the share of Western Europe rose from 34 to 60 percent.[44] Overall, Brazil avoided the classic colonial situation of overwhelming dependence on a single foreign market.[45]

It would be simplistic to analyze Brazil's political autonomy in exclusively economic terms. For example, as mentioned earlier, the last quarter of the nineteenth century was a period of intensified diplomatic collaboration between Brazil and the United States. This political activity occurred in the midst of the decline which we just

Table 4.7 *Share of Principal Markets for Brazil's Exports, 1840–1900* (in percent)

Market	1840	1860	1880	1900
United Kingdom	28	38	23	13
Other Western Europe	46	21	31	38
United States	23	29	44	43
Other	3	12	2	6

Source: Computed from data in John R. Hanson, 'The Nineteenth Century Exports of The Less Developed Countries' (PhD dissertation, University of Pennsylvania, 1972), pp. 321–4.

noted in the US share of Brazil's exports of coffee. As this case suggests, Brazil's position in the international political arena reflected more than its international economic situation. The geopolitical context and the political interests of the various powers were also pertinent. Nevertheless, the geographical diversification of Brazil's foreign trade cannot be ignored as a condition which facilitated a degree of national autonomy. Another fact is also pertinent here. Notwithstanding its heterodoxy in other policy areas, Brazil maintained the payments on its overseas debt, and thus gave foreign creditors no cause for intervention.[46]

The subject of Brazil's foreign-capital imports, however, raises other questions. It was not until the end of the century that Great Britain, the world's major capital-exporting country, supplied Brazil with investment resources which were large enough to have much impact on the country's economic development.[47] Consequently, one may ask: why did British capital take so *little* interest in Brazil before the 1890s? In addition to the implications for imperialist involvement, an earlier commitment of large-scale British investment might have done much to hasten Brazil's economic development. This is suggested by the data of Table 4.8. As the table indicates, the British capital that was invested in Brazil was allocated largely to the government and to infrastructure facilities. Infrastructure investments had major development effects in nineteenth-century Brazil. Similarly, by the last quarter of the century, the Brazilian state, too, was allocating an increasing share of its resources to promote the country's economic development.[48]

The contrast between Brazil's experience and that of the United States, where large sums of British capital were invested long before the 1890s, is striking. And as the case of the United States shows, a country did not have to be a British colony in order to have substantial British investment in the nineteenth century.[49] The small scale of British capital's involvement in Brazil cannot be explained (as has sometimes been proposed) by the fact that Great Britain was not a

Table 4.8 *Sectoral Composition of the Brazilian Capital Stock Financed by Public Securities Issued in London, 1885 and 1913* (in percent)

Sector	1885	1913
Government Loans	49	47
Railways	36	23
Public Utilities	6	22
Financial Institutions	—	4
Industrial and Miscellaneous	7	3
Raw Materials	2	1

Source: Computed from data in Irving Stone, 'The Geographical Distribution of British Investment in Latin America,' *Storia Contemporánea*, vol. 3 (September 1971), Table 5.

major consumer of coffee, and hence was not interested in lowering supply costs by expanding production in Brazil.[50] The returns to private foreign investors were fungible, and under the prevailing system of multilateral trade, there was no reason for returns from investments in Brazil to be linked to British commodity imports. Neither in coffee nor in other commodities did private British investors have to be concerned with externalities such as the impact of their investments on British import costs.

Further, special political risks, information costs, or capital-market imperfections can also not account for the relatively small flow of British capital to Brazil before the 1890s.[51] Finally, low private returns to foreign investment in Brazil are not a complete answer; for, in principle, the Brazilian government could have expanded its program of investment subsidies which supplemented private returns to foreign investors. In order to understand the magnitudes and timing of foreign investment in Brazil, then, we must also consider the conditions which determined the Brazilian government's efforts to promote the country's economic development. We will discuss that subject in the next chapter.

The Causes of Brazil's Delayed Industrial Development

Our earlier discussion suggests that imperialist pressures did not play a large role in Brazil's economic backwardness during the nineteenth century. That conclusion has important implications for the country's economic historiography. Some interpretations of Brazil's failure to industrialize earlier have in fact emphasized the 'imperialism of free trade' and the distorting economic and political forces present in the nineteenth-century world economy.[52] If imperialism does not account for Brazil's inability to industrialize earlier in the century, what were in fact the pertinent limitations? This question has been posed by other students of Brazil's economic history, particularly with respect to the delay in large-scale industrial development.[53] Brazil's industrial development began in the last half of the nineteenth century. But the size of the manufacturing sector remained too small – in terms of the share of GNP originating in industry or the fraction of the country's labor force which the industrial sector employed – to give a major impetus to the country's overall development.[54]

In reality, the issue of the delay in large-scale industrial development may not be as important as has often been assumed. As we have seen elsewhere, a more basic condition in Brazil's overall economic retardation was the failure of the domestic *agricultural* sector to achieve rising productivity during the nineteenth century.[55] Still, the issue of delayed industrialization has aroused considerable interest, both in Brazilian economic historiography and in the study of underdeveloped countries in general. As W. Arthur Lewis formulated the question:[56]

Why then did so little manufacturing industry develop in those tropical countries which were enriching themselves through agricultural exports? We may list seven possible explanations:

1. The destructive impact of foreign trade
2. The distribution of income
3. The use of political power by foreign traders
4. The need for infant industry protection
5. The absence of coal and iron ores
6. The superior profitability of agricultural exports
7. The absence of a domestic entrepreneurial class.

For the reasons discussed earlier, the first, third, and fourth explanations listed are not historically relevant for Brazil in the second half of the nineteenth century.[57] Moreover, tariff protection permitted rapid industrial growth to occur in Brazil despite the country's natural comparative advantage in agricultural exports.

Absence of a domestic entrepreneurial class would have constituted a handicap; for entrepreneurs were necessary to mobilize the capital, workers, and technology required for industrial development. In the Brazilian case, however, an ample supply of local entrepreneurs was present.[58] Relatedly, the supply of key inputs, for example, capital and skilled labor, proved to be relatively elastic once economic incentives for industrialization appeared.[59] It is also important to be clear about the economic effects of Brazil's highly skewed distribution of income in this context. Because of the low levels of per capita income which prevailed in nineteenth-century Brazil, the unequal distribution of income may in fact have promoted industrial development. Divided equally, the country's low income would have led perforce to a pattern of demand which was directed largely to food and other non-industrial products (see below). Unequal distribution, however, concentrated purchasing power in the hands of part of Brazil's population, and on a net basis probably enlarged the market for industrial products.[60]

One hypothesis which some writers have found convincing to explain Brazil's delay in large-scale industrialization is the country's lack of high-quality coal deposits.[61] This geological circumstance is alleged to have had two negative effects on Brazil's industrial development. First, it excluded metallurgical and engineering products from the range of goods produced in Brazil's early industrialization. Second, it reduced rates of return in other industrial activities, for they were obliged to use imported equipment and metallurgical goods. This interpretation, however, also suffers from some deficiencies. First, it neglects the possibilities for industrializing, as did Japan, on the basis of imported coal. Further, the impact of higher costs for imported capital goods on the returns to capital was at least partly offset by Brazil's low wage costs. Finally, the industrial products which were in demand at Brazil's low income levels were mainly food and fiber products. Consequently, the option of basing Brazilian industrialization on metallurgical and engineering products was in any case not historically relevant.[62]

Rather, the principal constraint on the emergence of large-scale industrial development in nineteenth-century Brazil seems to have been the small size of the domestic market for manufactured goods.[63] Per-capita income levels remained low through the century. And notwithstanding the skewed distribution of income, most expenditure in this economy went for food and other non-manufactures.[64] In addition to these income and Engel's curve effects, two other conditions also limited the size of the market for industrial products. Brazil's import duties permitted local producers to exceed world market prices in some products. But by increasing the relative price of manufactures, tariffs diminished domestic demand. Second, Brazil's large population was dispersed over a wide geographical area. The country's high internal transportation costs, too, raised the relative price of delivered manufactured goods, further limiting demand. Under these conditions, the demand for industrial products was too small to sustain a manufacturing sector that would generate a large percentage of national product or employ a noticeable fraction of the labor force in nineteenth-century Brazil.[65]

In such circumstances, large-scale Brazilian industrialization had to await the growth of the internal market which came with increasing domestic income and the expansion of low-cost transportation facilities. It is pertinent to observe that Brazil's links with the international economy were of central importance for both of these developments. The stimulus which export expansion gave to rising income in nineteenth-century Brazil is clear. And, as noted earlier, foreign investment and overseas borrowing by the Brazilian government were crucial for the railway construction which lowered internal transportation costs. This change helped promote the growth of income and demand for manufactures in Brazil's domestic agricultural sector.

Conclusions

Any interpretation which attributes to imperialism an important role in Brazil's slow economic development during the nineteenth century must confront some difficult historical facts. For example, Brazil's international terms of trade did not deteriorate during the century; they improved. Also, the returns to foreign capital do not seem to have been of a magnitude to drain a large volume of income overseas, and thus to impoverish Brazil. Indeed, until the end of the century, the marginal returns which foreign investors were able to obtain in Brazil were apparently too small to attract much international capital.

Other aspects of Brazil's historical experience also contradict the view that imperialism was an important obstacle to the country's development. On the contrary, integration into the growing world economy enabled Brazil to achieve rising income, a more capable state apparatus, and improved infrastructure facilities. These conditions, in turn, promoted Brazil's transition to more generalized economic development and domestic industrialization. Finally, our discussion raises doubts concerning the proposition that Brazil might have done better to follow an alternative development pattern based largely on domestically-oriented activities rather than on exports. In view of the conditions which prevailed in Brazil's domestic sector during the nineteenth century, that 'alternative' does not appear to have been historically available.

Imperialist control over Brazil's decision-making seems also to have been exaggerated as a factor in the country's poor economic experience. Even at the beginning of the period, British domination was not all-determining; Brazil was able to resist for almost half a century the external pressures to stop the importation of slaves. By the end of the century, Brazil had clearly increased its ability to withstand imperialist interference in determining its economic policies. Brazil was also able to avoid doctrinal dependence on the metropolitan powers. In practice, the country's fiscal, monetary, and exchange-rate policies were markedly heterodox. At the same time, Brazil's policies with respect to tariff protection, subsidized immigration, and coffee valorization also demonstrated the country's capacity for ideological and political autonomy. In this perspective, the 'informal empire' metaphor may obscure more than it illuminates about nineteenth-century Brazil.

More generally, as discussed elsewhere, internal rather than external conditions determined two of the central features of Brazil's macroeconomic experience during the nineteenth century: secular inflation and slow economic development.[66] Further, external political pressures are of little help in explaining the main cause of nineteenth-century Brazil's slow economic development – the failure to develop the domestic agricultural sector. Responsibility for that task necessarily lay with the Brazilian government, and it is hard to see how imperialism prevented the state from proceeding with this task.

In fact, when the Brazilian government did begin moving more energetically to develop the country with public investment programs, it found that access to the London financial market provided it with significant capital resources. In the last decades of the nineteenth century, Brazil's capital imports rose sharply.[67] At the same time, the Brazilian government began allocating an increasing share of its total expenditures for economic infrastructure. By 1913, the value of British investments in Brazilian government loans and railway securities amounted to some £179 million, or approximately £7.4 per Brazilian. These were sums which, in terms of contemporary prices and income levels can only be considered impressive.[68] Why it took so long before the Brazilian government undertook large-scale infrastructure programs is another question, to which we now turn.

Notes

1 See, for example, D. C. M. Platt, 'Dependency in Nineteenth-Century Latin America'; the 'Comment' by Stanley J. Stein and Barbara H. Stein; and the 'Reply' by Platt. These materials are in the *Latin American Research Review*, vol. 15 (November 1980), pp. 113–49. For a discussion of some of the issues, see Richard Graham, 'Robinson and Gallagher in Latin America: The Meaning of Informal Imperialism,' in William R. Louis (ed.), *Imperialism* (New York: 1976).

2 An early statement of this interpretation in the English language literature is presented in André Gunder Frank, 'The Capitalist Development of Underdevelopment in Brazil,' pp. 143–218 in his *Capitalism and Underdevelopment in Latin America: Historical Studies of Chile and Brazil* (New York: Monthly Review Press, 1967); and ibid., *Latin America: Underdevelopment or Revolution* (New York: Monthly Review Press, 1969), *passim*.

3 The tariff changes were formulated in the context of diplomatic conflict with the British government and, at least for some parties in Brazil, with overtly protectionist intent. On both points, see the details presented in Laura Randall, *A Comparative Economic History of Latin America, 1500–1914, Vol. 3. Brazil* (Ann Arbor: University Microfilms International, 1977), pp. 115–16. Similarly, R. Delson's reading of the British diplomatic papers for this period led her to the conclusion that Brazil's refusal to continue the low tariffs for imports from Great Britain started a deterioration of political relations which culminated with Britain's use of coercion to stop the importation of slaves to Brazil. See R. Delson, 'Sugar Production for the Nineteenth Century British Market: Rethinking the Roles of Brazil and the British West Indies' (mimeo., 1981). More generally, on Brazil's political-economic relations with Great Britain in this period, see Alan K. Manchester's *British Preeminence in Brazil: Its Rise and Decline* (Durham, NC: Duke University Press, 1933). That book's sub-title speaks volumes.

4 A. P. Lerner, 'The Symmetry Between Import and Export Taxes,' *Economica*, vol 3 (August 1936).

5 See pp. 168–76 in Chapter 8 of Nathaniel H. Leff, *Underdevelopment and Development in Brazil*, Vol. 1: *Economic Structure and Change, 1822–1947* (London: Allen & Unwin, 1982). Questions have been raised concerning whether import tariffs in Brazil during the second half of the nineteenth century were truly protective for domestic industry. Unfortunately this question has sometimes been addressed in terms of the claims by industrial spokesmen that they suffered from insufficient levels of protection. However, if we consider the rapid growth of industrial output (and the capacity to attract resources to import-competing manufacturing despite Brazil's strong comparative advantage in export agriculture), the answer to the question is evident. See also the discussion on pp. 211–3 of ibid., Chapter 9. Concerning Brazil's failure to achieve large-scale industrialization during this period, see pp. 87–9, below.

6 Celso Furtado has reached the same conclusion. See his *Formação Econômica do Brasil*, 5th edn (Rio de Janeiro: Fundo de Cultura, 1963), Chapter XVIII, pp. 121–2, and Chapter XIX, pp. 128–9. On another key point in this context, however, Furtado's interpretation seems questionable. Furtado suggested (pp. 121–2) that

the long-term (nominal) depreciation of the *mil-réis* during the nineteenth century afforded Brazilian producers protection against imports similar to what might have been provided by tariffs. That interpretation neglects an important consideration. Inflation in nineteenth-century Brazil involved a rise in domestic costs which was at least as great as the decline in the external value of the *mil-réis* (See Leff, *Economic Structure and Change*, op. cit., Chapter 6). Consequently, inflation and the associated currency depreciation gave Brazilian producers no net advantage in competing against import supply.

7   See Leff, *Economic Structure and Change*, op. cit., Chapter 8, pp. 165–71.

8   Ibid., Chapter 5, pp. 79–83. The data presented there relate to long-term trends. In addition, during some cyclical downturns in the world economy, the income terms of trade of Brazilian coffee exports also improved. See Table 2 of Carlos Manuel Peláez, 'The Theory and Reality of Imperialism in the Coffee Economy of Nineteenth-Century Brazil,' *Economic History Review* (May 1976).

9   Warren Dean, 'Remessas de Dinheiro dos Immigrantes Italianos do Brasil, Argentina, Uruguai, e Estados Unidos da America (1884–1914), *Anais de Historia*, vol. 6 (1974), esp. pp. 235–6.

10 See Leff, *Economic Structure and Change*, op. cit., Chapter 2, pp. 20–3.

11 Matthew Simon, 'The Pattern of New British Portfolio Foreign Investment, 1865–1914,' in John Adler (ed.) *Capital Movements and Economic Development* (New York: St. Martin's Press, 1967), p. 40. Long-term foreign investment from France, the second most important exporter of capital before 1914, showed a similar lack of interest in the colonies. Only 9 percent of French overseas investment went to the French Empire; 13 percent went to Latin America; and indeed, only 39 percent went to areas outside of Europe. These figures are computed from data in Herbert Feis, *Europe: The World's Banker: 1870–1914* (New Haven: Yale University Press, 1930), p. 51.

12 For documentation on these points, see E. Bradford Burns, *The Unwritten Alliance, Rio-Branco and Brazilian-American Relations* (New York: Columbia University Press, 1966), pp. 60–73.

13 On the strictly diplomatic plane, Brazil seems to have used its relation with the United States to consolidate its position within South America (Burns, *The Unwritten Alliance*, op. cit., pp. 199–209). When potential conflicts arose between Brazil and the United States, for example, in the claims of an American filibustering company in the Acre territory, the United States acceded to the Brazilian position (ibid., pp. 76–86). Consequently, it is hard to see how Brazil lost politically through its relation with the United States.

14 Leff, *Economic Structure and Change*, op. cit., Chapter 5.

15 On these points, see ibid., Chapter 7, pp. 144–53, and Chapter 9, pp. 194–6.

16 E. J. Chambers and D. F. Gordon, 'Primary Products and Economic Growth: An Empirical Measurement,' *Journal of Political Economy*, vol. 74 (August 1966).

17 See Leff, *Economic Structure and Change*, op. cit., Chapter 2, pp. 15–20.

18 On the close connection between export growth and the expansion of the Brazilian state's fiscal capacity see pp. 119–21 in Chapter 5, below.

19 See pp. 146–53 in Leff, *Economic Structure and Change*, op. cit., Chapter 7.

20 Ibid., Chapter 5.

21 Ibid., Chapters 8 and 9.

22 On these points, see Alan K. Manchester, *British Preeminence in Brazil*, op. cit., Chapters VII–XI.

23 José Jobson de Andrade Arruda has presented important new material on the gains which accrued to the Brazilian economy as a result of the ending of the Portuguese entrepôt monopoly. This material is contained in his 'O Brasil No Comércio Colonial, 1796–1808' (Tese de Doutoramento, Universidade de São Paulo, 1972), pp. 523–82.

24 See pp. 53–7 in Leff, *Economic Structure and Change*, op. cit., Chapter 4.

25 Karl Marx and Friedrich Engels, *The Communist Manifesto*, reprinted in T. B. Bottomore and M. Rubel, *Karl Marx, Selected Writings in Sociology and Social Philosophy* (London: Watts, 1961), pp. 136–8.

26 Nícia Vilela Luz, *A Luta Pela Industrialização do Brasil* (São Paulo: Difusão Européia do Livro, 1961), p. 104.

27 J. Pandiá Calógeras, *A Política Monetária do Brasil* (trans. by Thomaz Newlands Neto from the 1910 edition of *La Politique Monétaire du Brésil*) (São Paulo: Companhia Editora Nacional, 1961), p. 434.

28 Julian Duncan, *Public and Private Operation of Railways in Brazil* (New York: Columbia University Press, 1932), pp. 40–66.

29 Pierre Monbeig, *Pionniers et Planteurs de São Paulo* (Paris: Armand Colin, 1952), p. 99; Antônio Delfim Netto, 'Foundations for the Analysis of Brazilian Coffee Problems,' in Carlos Manuel Peláez (ed.), *Essays on Coffee and Economic Development* (Rio de Janeiro: Instituto Brasileiro do Café, 1973), p. 79.

30 See Celso Furtado, *Formação Econômica*, op. cit., Chapter 17, p. 117: 'Consequently one cannot conclude that if the Brazilian government had enjoyed complete freedom of action, the country's economic development would necessarily have been more rapid.'

31 By 'objective economic conditions,' I refer, for example, to the fact that after a rapid inflation like the *encilhamento* of the 1890s a program of monetary stabilization was necessary. Deflation would eventually have had to be implemented, regardless of the internal regime or external pressures.

32 This charge has often been raised against policy-makers in nineteenth-century Brazil. See, for example, Furtado, *Formação Econômica*, op. cit., Chapter 27, p. 187.

33 See, for example, José Arthur Rios, 'A Tradição Mercantilista na Formação Brasileira,' *Revista Brasileira de Economia*, vol. 26 (September 1972), esp. pp. 264–8.

34 Raymundo Faoro, *Os Donos do Poder*, 2nd edn (São Paulo, 1975), pp. 206–9, 222, 230. Similarly, on the pragmatism of private-sector interest groups, see Eugene W. Ridings, 'Interest Groups and Development: The Case of Brazil in The Nineteenth Century,' *Journal of Latin American Studies*, vol. 9 (1977), pp. 243–4.

35 Eulalia Lobo et al., 'Estudo das Categorias Socioprofisionais, dos Salarios, e do Custo de Vida no Rio de Janeiro de 1820 a 1930,' *Revista Brasileira de Economia*, vol. 29 (October 1973), pp. 139, 151–2.

36 In the last decades of the nineteenth century and early twentieth century, ideological currents which originated in Positivism oriented many leading policy-makers in an interventionist and relatively nationalist direction. This orientation was different from both classical liberalism and from contemporary socialist views. Most important here is that the Positivism which exerted an influence in Brazil was adapted pragmatically to local conditions. On these points, see R. G. Nachman, 'Positivism, Modernization, and The Middle Class in Brazil,' *Hispanic American Historical Review*, vol. 57 (January 1977), esp. pp. 12–18.

37 Some readers may wonder how appropriate it is in the context of nineteenth-century Brazil to speak of macroeconomic policies, with the implied connotations of self-conscious and purposive action. Our discussion here focuses on the pattern of behavior which government decisions traced out in various areas. Self-conscious or not, those patterns of government behavior constitute a policy.

38 These data relate to fiscal behavior under the Brazilian empire. For information on government budget deficits under post-1888 governments, see Leff, *Economic Structure and Change*, op. cit., Chapter 9, p. 194.

39 The discussion that follows in this paragraph is based on materials which are presented in Leff, *Economic Structure and Change*, op. cit., Chapter 6, pp. 108–13 and 120–1. Those materials also discuss the direction of causality between monetary expansion and exchange-rate depreciation in nineteenth-century Brazil.

40　As discussed in Leff, *Economic Structure and Change*, op. cit., Chapter 6 (pp. 111–3), nineteenth-century Brazil also experienced macroeconomic cycles around the trends in monetary expansion, inflation, and exchange depreciation. During these cycles, the degree of adherence to orthodox economic doctrine also waxed and waned. The long-term inflationary trends, however, constitute the principal structural feature in this context. These would not have been possible had Brazilian policy-makers followed monetary orthodoxy on a long-term basis.

41　See the discussion in Chapter 5, pp. 105–9, below.

42　Chapter 5, pp. 104–8, below.

43　D. C. M. Platt, *Latin America and British Trade, 1806–1914* (New York: Harper and Row, 1973), esp. Chapters VI–VIII.

44　These figures were computed from data in John Hanson, 'The Nineteenth Century Exports of the Less-Developed Countries' (PhD dissertation, University of Pennsylvania, 1972), p. 227.

45　Albert O. Hirschman, *National Power and Foreign Trade* (Berkeley: University of California Press, 1942).

46　Irving Stone, 'British Long-Term Investment in Latin America, 1865–1913,' *Business History Review*, vol. 42 (Autumn 1968), pp. 312–16.

47　See' Leff, *Economic Structure and Change*, op. cit., Chapter 7. As noted there, as late as 1885 British investment in Brazil amounted to only £48 million. In 1895, the figure was £93 million; and in 1913, £225 million. The relevant magnitude in the present context is the total stock of British investment in Brazil, not Brazil's share in British overseas investment or the percentage of British investment in total Brazilian capital formation.

48　See Chapter 5, below. The data of Table 4.8 refer only to capital transferred via loans or securities that were publicly issued. Consequently, British investment in manufacturing, which was sometimes made without such securities, is understated. On direct British investment in Brazilian industry during this period, see Richard Graham, *Britain and The Onset of Modernization in Brazil* (Cambridge University Press, 1968), pp. 142.

49　Conversely, for a country to be a British colony was not a sufficient condition for it to enjoy substantial capital inflow and development expenditure. See, for example, Gisela Eisner, *Jamaica, 1830–1930* (Manchester University Press, 1961), pp. 316–17.

50　See, for example, Warren Dean, *The Industrialization of São Paulo, 1880–1945* (Austin: University of Texas Press, 1969), pp. 46–7.

51　See Leff, *Economic Structure and Change*, op. cit., Chapter 7, pp. 136–7.

52　See, for example, Stanley J. Stein and Barbara H. Stein, *The Colonial Heritage of Latin America: Essays on Economic Dependence in Perspective* (New York: Oxford University Press, 1970).

53　See, for example, Furtado, *Formação Econômica*, op. cit., p. 122.

54　On these points, see Leff, *Economic Structure and Change*, op. cit., Chapter 8, pp. 172–3.

55　Ibid., Chapter 7.

56　W. Arthur Lewis, *Tropical Development, 1880–1913* (Evanston, Ill.: Northwestern University Press, 1970), p. 40.

57　These issues are discussed at greater length in Leff, *Economic Structure and Change*, op. cit., Chapter 5. One may also wonder about the possible effects of slavery as a constraint on Brazilian industrialization. On the supply side, it is not evident that slavery limited the country's industrial development. Indeed, slave-owners in nineteenth-century Brazil often found it worthwhile to train their slaves with marketable skills. Demand effects involve the level of the per capita consumption that was provided (directly and indirectly) to the slave population. Reflecting the income-distribution conditions discussed below, the per capita consumption of manufactured products by slaves was apparently low. Nevertheless, it is worth noting that, overall, the slave population constituted an important market for Brazilian industrialization. The coarse cotton textiles utilized by the slave population were one of the major products produced in the first decades of Brazilian industrialization.

58 Dean, *The Industrialization of São Paulo*, op. cit., Chapters II–IV.

59 See Leff, *Economic Structure and Change*, op. cit., Chapter 8, pp. 176–7.

60 Cf, Lewis, *Tropical Development*, op. cit., p. 41.

61 Lewis, *Tropical Development*, op. cit., pp. 41–3. See also Jean-Marie Martin, *Processus d'Industrialisation et Development Energetique du Brésil* (Paris: Institut des Hautes Etudes de l'Amerique Latine, 1966).

62 Cf. Charles P. Kindleberger's scepticism concerning the hypothesis that domestic coal supply conditions retarded the industrialization of France in the nineteenth century. That discussion is contained in his *Economic Growth in Britain and France, 1850–1960* (Cambridge, Mass.: Harvard University Press, 1964), pp. 17–29. If anything, an inelastic supply of coal would have been more important as a retarding factor in the French case; for, in view of the large difference in income levels, the pattern of demand was much more oriented toward coal-intensive products in nineteenth-century France than in Brazil.

63 Furtado has also stressed the small size of the domestic market as the central condition which limited early Brazilian industrialization. See his *Formação Econômica*, op. cit., Chapter 19, p. 128. The question of why Brazil did not overcome internal market constraints by exporting manufactures is discussed in Leff, *Economic Structure and Change*, op. cit., Chapter 8.

64 International cross-section estimates for the postwar period indicate that at per capita income levels between $100 and $300 (1963 prices), the same 80 percent of national income is spent on goods other than manufactures. This figure is from Table 9 of a paper by Dr. Michael Shefer, 'National Income and the Market for Manufactures' (Tel Aviv University, typescript, 1971). Shefer's figures for consumption of manufactures include both net value-added in the domestic manufacturing sector and the manufactured component of net imports. Shefer also presents data (pp. 28–36) which suggest that the regression plane that relates income levels to per capita consumption of manufactures has shifted outward over time. Hence the demand for manufactured products at given income levels was probably lower in the nineteenth century than in contemporary less-developed countries.

65 I have used the measures cited in the text as indices (rather than, say, the absolute size of the market for manufactured goods) for a special reason. We are focusing on industrialization as a source of productivity increase and development for the economy as a whole. Hence the need arises to scale the size of the industrial sector by the size of the economy. The empirical data that would be relevant here are figures on the consumption of manufactures as a percentage of aggregate income, C_{man}/Y. Such data are not available for nineteenth-century Brazil. The nearest measures available are figures which are related to the *per capita* consumption of manufactures, C_{man}/N. Divided by the level of per capita income (Y/N), this equals C_{man}/Y.

In the 1850s, Brazil's per capita imports from Great Britain, the country's major supplier of manufactured goods, amounted to some $2.3 per annum. In the 1870s, the figure was still less than $3.2. (These numbers were computed from data in Graham, *Britain and the Onset of Industrialization*, op. cit., pp. 330–3.) Allowing for manufactures which came from other suppliers, and making assumptions on the plausible level of Y/N in Brazil at the time, these figures do not imply a figure for C_{man}/Y which would have been sufficient to sustain large-scale industrialization.

66 Leff, *Economic Structure and Change*, op. cit., Chapters 6 and 7.

67 Concerning the general phenomenon discussed here, see Leff, *Economic Structure and Change*, op. cit., Chapter 7, Table 7.4. The figure cited later in this paragraph is from Stone, 'British Long-Term Investment,' op. cit., pp. 325–9.

68 One may wonder about the extent to which this degree of foreign-capital inflow forced Brazil into a pattern of economic and political dependency in the decades following 1913. That question is addressed in Leff, *Economic Structure and Change*, op. cit., Chapter 9.

5
Government

Introduction

We have not yet given sustained attention to a topic which is of obvious importance – the role of Brazil's government in the country's economic experience during the nineteenth century. The intrinsic historic interest of this topic is clear; and, in addition, this is also a subject of general relevance. Questions concerning the relations between government and economic development have aroused considerable discussion, both among casual observers and among social scientists. This topic is important because the state can influence the pace and direction of a country's economic expansion in many ways.[1] In addition to its classical role of ensuring political integration and stability, government action may change relative prices in the product and factor markets. Further, public investment which provides external economies can also raise private rates of return and capital formation. This chapter considers the impact of government action on economic development in nineteenth-century Brazil.

Before beginning the discussion, some clarifying comments are necessary. First, this chapter focuses mainly on government action in the area of economic policy. A full-scale analysis of politics in nineteenth-century Brazil is beyond the scope of the present study, and is in any case better left to specialists in that subject. For our purposes, it suffices to note that socioeconomic groups such as the large landowners and the export producers had considerable power and influence.[2] At the same time, the political-bureaucratic elite who comprised the high echelons of the state apparatus also had some scope for politically autonomous action.[3] Second, we cannot discuss here the details of Brazilian economic policy during the nineteenth century. However, within the broad perspective of long-term economic development, we can discuss some central features of what the government did (and did not do) to promote the country's economic progress. That discussion leads us to consider the budgetary conditions which constrained the level of government developmental activity. And that focus obliges us to devote considerable attention later in this chapter to a topic which might otherwise appear unimportant – public finance in Brazil during the nineteenth century.

Some Features of Brazilian Government Policy

The Brazilian state was relatively effective in its integrative role of holding the country together. From independence through the 1840s, there were numerous uprisings against the central government. These challenges sometimes involved serious costs for the imperial regime. Nevertheless, the government and the informal political system were able to deal with these threats without disruptive armed strife of the magnitude which afflicted some other Latin American countries during the nineteenth century.[4] Thus the Brazilian state provided the modicum of political stability necessary for investment and production to proceed with minimal interference. In addition, the state maintained private property rights in the more densely-settled areas. (In the more distant regions, property rights were generally assured by the local overlord's monopoly of violence.) The Brazilian state was also able to cope successfully with threats of secession and territorial fragmentation. Indeed, in the case of the Northeast, from a narrow economic view the imperial regime may have been *too* successful in this regard.[5] Finally, with its gradualist policies, the government spared Brazil a cataclysmic political crisis in dealing with the conflict engendered by the pressures for abolition of slavery.

The contrast between Brazil's relative political stability and the more common Latin American pattern was partly due to the way in which the shift from the colonial regime to national independence came in Brazil. The transition occurred without a challenge to traditional criteria for political legitimacy, and without a military mobilization and generals who subsequently contended for *jefe maximo* (supreme leader) roles.[6] Those conditions might have generated chronic political instability in Brazil's post-independence period, as they did in the former Spanish American colonies. A change in Portugal's colonial policies during the decades preceding independence seems to have facilitated the relatively smooth transition in Brazil. Imperial reform and cooptation of Brazilian elites eased the shift to the post-independence regime.[7] Thereafter, long-term political stability was promoted by the process with which the political leadership was socialized and deployed in Brazil. The pattern that was developed led to the formation of a relatively homogeneous political class which was oriented to national unity and stable civilian government.[8]

Another important area of government action was macroeconomic policy. This involved the state's activities in the monetary, fiscal, and exchange-rate realm. The measures adopted here were generally conducive to expansionary aggregate demand. Supply conditions, however, were relatively inelastic in this economy.[9] Inelastic supply was especially pronounced for domestic foodstuffs, because of the poor transportation conditions which prevailed in the interior until the end of the century. Under these circumstances, buoyant aggregate demand led to chronic price inflation in nineteenth-century Brazil. And it is not at all clear that inflation promoted the country's economic development.

Government actions also affected the allocation of resources between activities in Brazil's economy. The policies which raised tariffs against some manufactured imports in the second half of the century helped promote Brazil's industrial development.[10] And the duties imposed on imported foodstuffs toward the end of the nineteenth century stimulated growth in the Southeast's domestic agricultural sector. Brazil's export taxes had similar economic effects in directing resources to the economy's import-competing activities.[11] It is worth noting that Brazil rejected unqualified reliance on free trade and liberal orthodoxy decades before such doctrinal liberation seems to have occurred in other Latin American countries.[12]

Discussion has often focused on the policies which had a direct impact on the composition of aggregate output in Brazil (e.g. industrialization). But government actions in other domains also had important effects on the economy's expansion pattern. These were the policy measures which changed the availability and relative prices of the factors of production – land, labor, and capital. By influencing relative factor prices, government policy affected the techniques employed, the returns to the different factors of production, and the distribution of income. The main thrust of Brazilian policy here was to increase the supply of labor relative to the other factors, and to limit access of small-holders to land.

When Brazil achieved independence, in 1822, much of the land near the settled regions had already been allocated to private latifundists. Consequently, unlike the situation in the United States, the central government did not have at its disposal a large quantity of economic land which it could make available to small- and medium-scale settlers. It is equally clear, however, that Brazilian land policy did little to encourage break-up of the large estates and sale of small parcels, with credit and secure tenure, to non-latifundists. Continuing imperfections in the land and capital markets also facilitated oligopsony in local labor markets. Another theme in Brazilian government policy throughout the century was its emphasis on maintaining an elastic supply of low-cost labor.[13] This concern is evident in the government's resistance to British pressures against the overseas importation of slaves. And when the British finally forced a stop to the traffic, a change which might have led eventually to a rise in domestic labor costs, Brazilian governments promoted the importation of low-cost workers from Europe. These policies permitted labor to continue as a relatively abundant factor in the Brazilian economy. By affecting the country's factor endowment in this manner, government measures raised the returns to capital and to land.

This policy orientation comes as no surprise in a society where the government was very sensitive to the planter and landholding interests. However, it does caution us against adopting a naive view on the role of government in promoting economic development. That would be a perspective in which it is assumed that the state acts to overcome the economic problems which afflict a society because markets are incomplete or fail to operate effectively. As we have just seen, the government may indeed act to resolve economic problems – but those of a specific class rather than those of society as a whole. Further, overcoming one group's problems may aggravate those of another. The use, by the planter class, of the state apparatus to maintain an elastic flow of low-cost labor from overseas may have answered to the needs of the planters; but it also depressed the incomes of Brazilian workers.

The foregoing discussion can readily be summarized. During the nineteenth century, the Brazilian state acted relatively ably in its integrative role, holding the country together. From the perspective of its special class underpinnings, the state also performed capably in influencing the country's relative factor returns and the distribution of income. In one area, however, the Brazilian state was much less effective: it did not succeed in providing the country with an adequate stock of social overhead capital. By generating external economies, an increased supply of socioeconomic infrastructure might well have facilitated a more rapid pace of aggregate capital formation and economic development.[14]

With the conditions that prevailed in nineteenth-century Brazil, it would have been especially helpful if the government had promoted large-scale investment in transportation much earlier than actually occurred.[15] In particular, there are reasons to believe that the positive effects of railways in lowering the costs of shipping bulky, low-value commodities, and thereby promoting the development of Brazil's domestic agricultural sector during the nineteenth century would have been substantial. Partly because of this reason, the social returns of transportation investment often exceeded the private financial returns which the railways yielded to their owners. Note, moreover, that major differences existed between Brazil and the United States with respect to the availability of low-cost transportation *sans* railroads. In the pre-railroad era, the United States possessed much more ample transportation facilities to its hinterland (e.g. better roads, navigable, interconnecting waterways, and canals). Because these alternative modes of transportation in the interior were available, the importance of the railways for the economic development of the United States has been questioned. In Brazil, however, transportation costs in the pre-railroad era were much higher, and the impact of the railroads was correspondingly greater. In fact, the extension of the country's railways seems to have been a key factor in the onset of a more generalized pattern of development in Brazil toward the end of the nineteenth century.

Further, in the United States, much social overhead capital was provided by market institutions or by voluntary associations. In Brazil, however, the relative absence of external economies lowered the private returns to efforts by such agencies, and gave a special significance to promotional activity by the government. Moreover, the need for public-sector *investment* programs was especially great because there were distinct limits to what the government could achieve via promotional legislation. Thus Brazil had a modern railway law by the mid-1830s. Large-scale railway construction, however, did not come for decades. Similarly, in 1850 the government made major changes in the country's Commercial Code, modernizing the treatment of incorporation and of property rights. This legislative reform did not stimulate widespread economic development. And the introduction to the Northeast of institutional provisions similar to those which Torrens had pioneered in Australia was insufficient to generate a similar pattern of agricultural development. Because important structural changes in the Brazilian economy during the nineteenth century often required public-sector investment, the failure of the Brazilian state in this area had unusual importance for the country's economic experience. And for this reason, the causes of the government's inadequate investment performance during the nineteenth century merit special attention.

Some Possible Explanations

Even when asking why something did *not* happen, one must respect history's basic fabric and internal consistency. Accordingly, the question here is not why the Brazilian state did not launch a massive development effort along lines familiar from the post-Second World War epoch. Rather, the issue is the failure of the state to embark earlier in the century on a public-sector investment and subsidy program similar to the policies that were actually implemented in Brazil toward the end of the century. That program was sufficient to accelerate the pace of the country's economic development significantly. Why did it not occur, say, half a century earlier? A number of explanations come to mind.

It may be suggested that ideological constraints, such as an undue deference to *laissez-faire* doctrines, prevented the state from taking a more active promotional role in the economy. In accordance with this interpretation, Brazilian policy-makers have sometimes been portrayed as culturally alienated, and subservient to orthodox economic ideologies developed elsewhere but inappropriate for a country like

Brazil. In fact, however, this explanation is not relevant in this historical case. As we saw in Chapter 4, Brazil's political elite often displayed considerable heterodoxy in its economic policies. The state also intervened directly in the economy to subsidize steamboats for coastal shipping, railway construction (on a limited scale), sugar mills in the Northeast, and European immigration. Although advocates of *laissez-faire* orthodoxy were often heard in nineteenth-century Brazil, the reality of government policy was usually very different.

Another explanation suggests that it would be anachronistic to expect that the Brazilian state in the nineteenth century would manifest an interest in economic development. The country's political and administrative elite are generally considered to have been more interested in self-aggrandizement and bureaucratic expansion than in economic development. Such concerns, however, are perfectly consistent with a vastly enlarged promotional role for the public sector. Expanded state investment and subsidy programs would have meant more governmental jobs, and greater control over society's economic resources. Thus the existence of self-seeking motives is hardly an adequate explanation of the state's failure to pursue a more active development policy.

One might also propose internal political conditions as the distortion which prevented implementation of a rational infrastructure policy. The large landowners exerted considerable influence over Brazilian economic policy-making during the nineteenth century. And Brazil's landowners are generally not considered to have been a very progressive or developmentally-oriented group. Far from explaining the failure of Brazilian governments to provide larger infrastructure investments, however, such a 'political' explanation only sharpens the question. For, following Schumpeter's insight concerning the convergence of monopoly and socialism, one would expect large landowners to be especially energetic in pressing for public investment.[16] This is because landowners with extensive holdings and market power can internalize and appropriate most of the social benefits of infrastructure investment. Indeed, with a small number of very large landowners, the availability of public goods should be closer to the social optimum than in a more egalitarian society, for the returns to individual participation in public affairs are greater.[17] Consequently, Brazil's social stratification and internal political conditions should have led to *large* government investments in economic infrastructure.

Brazil's socioeconomic elites were clearly well-placed to take the lion's share of the benefits from increased investment in economic infrastructure. Nevertheless, the country's dominant elites might in principle have objected to accelerated economic development because of another reason – concern that such a process would lead to the loss of their social and political predominance.

As attractive as this interpretation may appear, it is not very relevant in the Brazilian historical context. Brazil's elites began the century with ample means to assure their political and social position; and they retained undisputed control throughout the period. In addition to the usual techniques for maintaining elite dominance, a special feature which facilitated social and political stability in Brazil was the elastic supply of workers from overseas. This inflow kept labor abundant (and cheap) relative to capital, in a great constant of Brazil's history during the nineteenth century. In fact, when accelerated infrastructure investment and economic advance did eventually come to Brazil, the stabilizing factors we have noted did operate; and the country's elites were able to maintain their predominance without challenge. As history was to demonstrate, economic expansion and structural change could occur in Brazil with minimal alteration in the fundamental relations of power. It is hard to see why the social and political ramifications of economic change would have been different if a similar process had been launched decades earlier.

Demand and Supply of Government Development Activity

For the reasons indicated, we must seek other answers to the question of why the Brazilian government did not play a larger role in investment and supply of infrastructure for economic development during most of the nineteenth century. Note, however, that as conventionally posed, this question involves a classical identification problem. To what extent was the government's failure due primarily to conditions on the 'demand' side – the pressures for economic development which made themselves felt in terms of the current ideology and political regime? And to what extent was it due to conditions on the 'supply' side – a lack of the financial, administrative, and intellectual resources necessary to implement a large infrastructure program? For the sake of analytical clarity, we must discriminate between these two distinct sets of influences.

'Demand' conditions do not seem to have been the major problem. This is suggested by the fact that nineteenth-century Brazilian governments did implement measures, for example, subsidies for European immigration and for technological modernization in Northeast sugar production, which were believed to be developmental but which did not require a large resource input on its part. As noted earlier, in a country dominated by large landowners, the presence of favorable demand conditions for developmental policies is readily understandable. It may be suggested, however, that landowners in the plantation regions opposed the building of railroads to the interior of Brazil. This is because railway construction created a new source of demand for workers, and might thus have raised the planters' labor costs. Upward pressure on wages might also occur as railways lowered the cost to the planters' workers of migration to the abundant lands in Brazil's interior. In fact, however, these private considerations which might have militated against railway construction do not appear applicable in the Brazilian case. The elastic supply of imported labor (which was maintained through the use of other policies) effectively shielded the planters from long-term upward pressures on wages. Further, lower transport costs from the interior might well have *reduced* the planters' wage costs. This is because the railways lowered the supply curve for (wage-good) foodstuffs. At the same time, the railroads also increased that supply curve's elasticity with respect to price.[18] 'Demand' conditions, then, do not seem to have been the dominant constraint which limited the scale of the government's infrastructure programs.

If we turn to consider the supply of inputs necessary for a larger government development program, intellectual resources do not seem to have been the major problem. Obviously Brazil's political elites perceived the country's economic needs strictly within the framework of their own class interests. As noted above, income-distributional concerns ranked high within that perspective. Within its own framework, however, the leadership seems in general to have been intellectually aware of what was necessary for (their version of) the country's economic development. And as we have seen, expanded provision of economic infrastructure would have served the interests of Brazil's elites. Further, the country's political leaders were also willing to depart from some current doctrinal orthodoxies to implement measures they deemed necessary. Intellectual comprehension of the situation, however, was not a sufficient condition for economic development. Thus, the country had a modern railroad law by the 1830s, but that alone was not enough to stimulate large-scale railroad construction.

The major instance where an intellectual hiatus appears to have hampered economic development occurred in the case of the Northeast. As we saw in Chapter 2, in order to develop more rapidly, the Northeast required a *mil-réis*/sterling parity that was consistently higher than the country's overall exchange rate. Unfortunately, the technology of multiple exchange rates had not yet been invented in the nineteenth century. Consequently, the failure of Brazil's elite in this case is understandable. By contrast, the country's political leadership was sufficiently innovative toward the end of the period to devise and implement the valorization program which was used to raise the value of coffee exports.

If we continue the search for constraints on the supply of government promotional activity in nineteenth-century Brazil, one factor becomes readily apparent – public finance. Until the last decades of the nineteenth century, the fiscal resources which the Brazilian state had available to pay for infrastructure investment and subsidy programs were small relative to the country's development needs. The public-finance constraint on government spending, in turn, stemmed from two underlying conditions. The state felt compelling pressures to allocate resources for purposes other than economic development. In addition, the level of *total* government spending was relatively low.

As discussed below, an explanation in these terms resolves the basic problem we have posed concerning the government's inadequate promotional role in nineteenth-century Brazil. However, this explanation also raises a further question. If public expenditure on social overhead capital would have generated large net benefits, and if the country's oligarchy would have appropriated the greater part of these benefits, why did Brazil's socioeconomic elites not provide the tax resources necessary to finance a higher level of infrastructure investment? The answer to that question will occupy us later in this chapter. First, however, it is necessary to consider some quantitative dimensions of Brazilian public finance during the nineteenth century.

The Public-Finance Constraint on Development Spending

Table 5.1 presents data on the central government's expenditures in successive decades of the nineteenth century. These figures tell much about total spending of Brazil's overall public sector, for during most of the century the country's fiscal system was highly centralized. Until the 1880s, the tax revenues of the central government were approximately 4.5 times greater than those of the provincial governments.[19] The share of the central government in total public-sector *expenditure* was even larger, for the central government had much greater access to foreign and domestic borrowing. Some fiscal decentralization occurred after 1891, but, even so, until 1913 the central government's tax revenues remained some three times larger than those of the provinces. In a similar fashion, the revenues collected by local governments in nineteenth-century Brazil also amounted to only a small fraction of total public-sector revenue.[20] Hence, the data in Table 5.1 provide an important indicator of the level and growth of total public-sector expenditure during the century.

As Table 5.1 indicates, the Brazilian state's level of expenditures was relatively low during most of the nineteenth century. Total annual expenditures remained below £5 million (approximately $25 million) until the Paraguayan War of the 1860s. And as late as the 1890s, annual spending by the central government amounted to less than £15 million (approximately $75 million).

We will discuss below some features of the fiscal system that yielded the low levels (and the upward trend) which are apparent in Table 5.1. Here, however, note that the financial resources available to Brazil's

Table 5.1 *The Sterling Value of Central Government Expenditure in Nineteenth-Century Brazil, Current and Constant Sterling Prices*

(1) Period	(2) Average Annual Expenditure in Current Sterling Prices (thousands of £)	(3) Expenditure per capita in Current Prices (£)	(4) Average Annual Expenditure in Constant (1880) Sterling Prices (thousands of £)	(5) Expenditure per capita in Constant (1880) Prices (£)
1823–31	1,747	.344	999	.196
1832–41	2,377	.401	1,703	.286
1842–51	3,170	.460	2,918	.423
1852–61	4,919	.614	4,534	.566
1862–71	10,051	1.075	7,923	.846
1872–81	13,769	1.252	12,483	1.128
1882–91	14,873	1.113	16,973	1.268
1892–1901	14,679	.887	18,146	1.097
1902–11	29,609	1.409	33,519	1.598

Source: Computed from data on the *mil-réis* value of central government expenditure which are presented in Oliver Ónody, *A Inflação Brasileira, 1822–1958* (Rio de Janeiro, 1960), pp. 195–8, and from data on the Brazilian exchange rate. To compute the value of the central government's expenditure in constant sterling prices, the export price index of the United Kingdom, Brazil's major source of imports, was used. This series is from Albert H. Imlah, *Economic Elements in The Pax Britannica* (Cambridge, Mass.: Harvard University Press 1958), pp. 94–8.

central government appear even more meager if they are expressed relative to the size of the population whose welfare they might have been used to promote. Per capita expenditure figures are presented in columns (3) and (5) of Table 5.1. As these data indicate, for the first four decades after independence, per capita government spending was well below £1. It was only with the Paraguayan War that per capita expenditure exceeded £1. And it was not until the first decade of the twentieth century that central government expenditure in current prices approached £1.5 per capita.

Different measuring rods can be used to assess these expenditure levels. The Brazilian figures might be compared, for example, with the magnitude of government spending in contemporary less-developed countries. We might also compare government expenditure levels in Brazil with those prevailing in the United States during the nineteenth century. However, our primary interest here is not in a comparative study of public finance. In the present context, the most pertinent comparison is the magnitude of the government's fiscal resources relative to the size of the development task which Brazil faced in the nineteenth century. The country's initial conditions with respect to social overhead capital were poor.[21] At the same time, difficult geographical and topographical conditions meant that the costs of providing a useable transportation system were high. Viewed in these terms, the financial resources available to the Brazilian state until the end of the nineteenth century appear to have been relatively small.

The possibilities for a public-sector investment program that would have had a large development impact were also hampered by another condition. During much of the nineteenth century, claimants other than economic development absorbed a large portion of the Brazilian state's total financial resources. Table 5.2 shows the uses to which aggregate central government expenditure was put in selected years from 1840 to 1889.

Some explanation of the five categories utilized in Table 5.2 may be helpful. The 'Administrative' category relates mainly to the personnel expenditures of the various government ministries. In view of the special interest concerning military expenditures, the allocations to the military ministries are grouped separately. Further, debt service is listed as a special item because of the pre-emptive priority which Brazilian governments accorded to amortization and interest payments on the country's foreign and domestic debt. Finally, 'Economic Development' comprises government expenditures for such purposes as public works, health and education, steam navigation, and railways.

Table 5.2 shows several important features. First, expenditure for administrative and military purposes accounted for a relatively large portion of central government spending in the initial years of the period. Over time, however, the percentage of these two expenditure categories fell perceptibly. Thus the share of administrative and military expenditure declined from 72 percent of central government expenditure in 1841–42 to 35 percent in 1889. The long-term decline was especially marked (with the exception of the Paraguayan War years) for the share of military spending. Second, Table 5.2 shows that at the beginning of the period and through most of the century,

Table 5.2   *Allocation of Central Government Expenditures by Use, 1841–1889* (in percent)

Years	Administra- tive	Military	Debt Service	Miscel- laneous	Economic Development
1841–42	19	53	17	3	8
1845–46	21	49	20	5	5
1850–51	41	27	18	4	10
1859–60	20	47	14	3	16
1865–66	13	67	9	3	8
1870–71	16	34	26	4	20
1880–81	12	19	29	14[a]	26
1889	12	23	27	5	33

[a] The relatively large share of the 'Miscellaneous' category in 1880–81 reflects exceptionally high expenditures on ex-slaves in those years.

Source: Computed from data in José Murilo de Carvalho, 'Elite and State Building in Imperial Brazil' (PhD dissertation, Stanford University, 1974), pp. 578, 580, 581.

spending for economic development accounted for only a small portion of total central government expenditure. Apart from the war years, however, the trend in this category was upward. By 1889 the share of development expenditure had risen to 33 percent of the total.

Two basic conditions, then, explain the public-finance constraint on the Brazilian state's capacity to provide the country with more adequate economic infrastructure until the end of the nineteenth century. The government's financial resources were small relative to the country's development needs; and the share of development spending in overall central government expenditure was low during most of the period. These conditions, however, were only the proximate causes of the problem. In order to understand the situation more completely, we must consider the underlying factors which determined both the initial severity and the subsequent relaxation of the public-finance constraint on development spending in nineteenth-century Brazil.

Government Allocation Patterns

The reasons for the governmental allocation pattern shown in Table 5.2 are straightforward. The Brazilian government gave a high priority to maintaining political stability and avoiding territorial secession; and the military and the bureaucratic apparatus were the major policy instruments which the state utilized for those purposes. Note further that if one places a high value on political integration, one cannot also fault the Brazilian government for allocating expenditure to achieve that objective. Political stability is a public good whose importance for economic development has long been recognized. And maintenance of territorial integrity was evidently valued highly on non-economic grounds. North Americans who consider excessive the emphasis which Brazilian governments placed on integrative activities may recall the heavy costs incurred in the United States Civil War.[22]

More generally, the high priority which the Brazilian state gave to holding the country together fits a pattern observed by Bert Hoselitz.[23] He suggested that new states concentrate first on political integration, and only later focus on other problems such as economic development. Those priorities are understandable. However, the relatively large share of Brazilian government expenditure that was spent on political integration did have an important side-effect. Because of this allocation pattern, during most of the century the resources available for public-sector investment in development projects were even smaller than might appear from the low absolute levels of government expenditure shown in Table 5.1.

In the course of the nineteenth century, the composition of central-government expenditures in Brazil underwent a marked shift. The portion of spending that was allocated for integrative activities fell, and the share for economic development rose (see Table 5.2). Moreover, the latter trend continued after the 1880s, the data for which are shown in Table 5.2. Information on the composition of central government expenditure from 1890 to 1913 indicates that the share of *fixed* capital formation increased from an annual average of 7 percent in the 1890s to 11 percent in the 1900s. By the years 1910–13, the portion had risen to 21 percent.[24]

Four (complementary) hypotheses might explain this shift in the composition of central government spending in nineteenth-century Brazil. First, the preferences and values of the country's political leadership may have changed. In response to new ideological currents, they may have begun to accord a higher priority to economic development. Alternatively, preferences did not change; but rather economic development was a 'luxury' good for the country's elites. Hence, even with unchanging preferences, the government allocated a larger proportion of expenditure to development as total spending reached higher absolute levels.

Another possibility is that the institutions and habits that were developed in the earlier period of more intensive state-building had had a cumulative and intertemporal effect. Consequently, in later years, the same level of political tranquility could be achieved with proportionally lower spending for integrative purposes. Finally, some expenditures for integrative purposes may have had 'fixed cost' aspects. That is, once certain threshold levels were reached (e.g. with respect to troop levels), economies of scale occurred. Accordingly, similar political results could be achieved without proportionate increases in government expenditures.

Presenting these four hypotheses may help us avoid an overly facile approach to explaining the shift in the Brazilian government's allocation pattern during the nineteenth century. An examination of their relative merits, however, would take the present discussion too far afield. Moreover, whatever may have been the causes of the shift, its effect in the present context is clear: to make available additional resources for public-sector investment. Coming together with the rise in total government expenditure, the allocational change led to a pattern of accelerating government spending for economic development toward the end of the century.

The Constraint on Overall Fiscal Resources

The other major factor which determined the small scale of public-sector investment during most of the nineteenth century was the low overall level of Brazilian government expenditure. This condition reflected some basic features of the fiscal situation which confronted the Brazilian state in its effort to raise tax revenues. In economically advanced countries, the demand for public-sector services is usually a major determinant of the volume of government expenditures. In underdeveloped countries, by contrast, public-finance levels are often determined by supply constraints – the paucity of tax bases that yield revenues commensurate with the costs of tax collection.[25] That is, conditions which typically prevail in underdeveloped countries (see below) may lead to prohibitively high collection costs for incremental tax revenues. Consequently, government spending does not reach the scale that would be socially optimal if such 'transactions costs' did not have to be considered.

Such a rigidity seems to have constrained public-finance levels in nineteenth-century Brazil. As noted earlier, the Brazilian state had major incentives (if only for the sale of its own self-aggrandizement) to enlarge the volume of economic resources at its disposal. The country's landowners, who would have appropriated most of the benefits from expanded public-sector investment, also stood to gain. However, a sharp increase in fiscal penetration within the broader society also involved significant economic costs. Consequently, the net marginal social benefits of public-finance expansion were very low. As a result, such fiscal expansion understandably (and rationally) encountered resistance on the part of Brazil's socioeconomic elites.

Because of the great distances, poor communications, and low literacy rates in this vast agrarian country, the costs involved in reaching most potential tax bases were high. By contrast, taxes on imports and exports were relatively easy to collect. For this reason, the Brazilian government's revenues and expenditures depended heavily on foreign-trade duties. Between 1830 and 1885, some 70 percent of the state's revenues came from taxes on imports and exports.[26] As this figure indicates, generalized taxes on agricultural land were not an important source of government revenue in nineteenth-century Brazil. In this respect, the country contrasted notably with countries like India or Japan during the nineteenth century.[27] The political power of Brazil's landowners does not appear to be the pertinent explanation of this difference. Import and export duties *were* levied on the foreign-trade sector, which included the country's most powerful landholders. And as noted earlier, the large landowners would have appropriated most of the gains from a situation in which the benefits of higher government investment spending exceeded the costs. In view of these conditions, a more complex explanation is necessary to explain the absence of generalized land taxation in Brazil.

One circumstance which is relevant in this context was Brazil's abundance of land, and the ensuing low ratios of labor to land in the country's domestic agricultural sector. With little Malthusian pressure of population on land, Ricardian rent, the base for land taxation, was low.[28] This feature of meager rent has often been discussed in terms of financial illiquidity. However, low net income was the more pertinent underlying condition. Further, poor communications and low literacy rates in Brazil meant that the administrative costs of levying a land tax were high. (Cadastral surveys were of course only part of these administrative costs.) These conditions which made for high trans-actions costs and a low economic surplus meant that the net fiscal yields generated by generalized taxation of land in Brazil's domestic agri-cultural sector would have been small. By contrast, scarcity of land in some Asian countries led to a situation in which Ricardian rents were sufficiently large to provide a major source of tax revenues and public-sector expenditure.

In Brazil's foreign-trade sector, however, circumstances were very different. There, transactions costs were not so large relative to the size of the economic surplus as to lower sharply the net social gains of taxation. Because of these differences between Brazil's foreign-trade sector and the domestic agricultural sector, then, government revenues and spending in nineteenth-century Brazil depended heavily on the size of the country's international trade receipts. The tax rates imposed on this base could not be set at arbitrarily high levels, however, lest exports and imports diminish to the point where total tax revenues would fall. Unfortunately, through most of the nineteenth century, the value of Brazil's foreign trade was too small to provide a large volume of fiscal resources. A comparative perspective from the nineteenth-century United States is useful in this context. The central government in the United States also relied heavily on import duties as a source of tax revenue during the nineteenth century. But the value of foreign trade in the United States was so much greater than in Brazil that it provided a vastly superior tax base.[29]

The Brazilian state attempted to supplement its tax revenues by borrowing, both at home and abroad. In 1864, before the Paraguayan War, government debt amounted to £2.1 per person in Brazil.[30] In 1870, after the sharp increase in wartime expenditures and borrowing, the figure was £4.1. Moreover, the Brazilian government's borrowing was not limited to foreign sources. Between 1841 and 1889, the share of domestically-held obligations in total government debt-service pay-ments ranged from 42 to 62 percent.[31] Although borrowing afforded the Brazilian state a welcome short-term addition to its fiscal resources, it did not solve the country's public-finance problems. Indeed, debt service came to constitute a major claimant on government expendi-ture (see Table 5.2). Further, the scope for borrowing was set ulti-mately by debt-service capacity, and hence by tax revenues. During most of the nineteenth century, these did not permit a high level of per capita government expenditure in Brazil.

The Growth of Government Fiscal Resources

Our discussion has stressed the importance of Brazil's foreign trade as the predominant source of the government's revenues during the nineteenth century. The underlying tax base in this fiscal system was exports, which provided an opportunity for levying export taxes. Also, the imports which exports made possible opened the possibility for collecting import duties. In addition, higher exports increased the state's capacity to borrow. And finally, export growth had an indirect impact in stimulating the expansion of urban (and perhaps also of some rural) activities which could be taxed at a relatively low cost. These considerations may be plausible in *a priori* terms. But it is essential to ascertain whether an approach which emphasizes the role of exports in nineteenth-century Brazil's public finance is consistent with the empirical data and Brazil's actual historical experience. That experience involved a long-term expansion in the country's public finances (see Table 5.1). Thus, between 1822 and 1913, the central government's expenditure, expressed in nominal *mil-réis*, rose at a trend rate of 4.8 percent per annum. In per capita terms, the government's nominal expenditure grew at an annual rate of 3.1 percent. (The growth of government spending in real terms was of course lower to the extent that Brazil experienced long-term price inflation during the nineteenth century.[32])

Two basic questions stand out for empirical testing. To what extent does the growth of Brazil's foreign trade during the nineteenth century explain, in statistical terms, the fiscal expansion of the Brazilian state during this period? Also, one would like to know by *how much* did the growth of exports lead to an expansion of central government expenditures or receipts? To answer that question we must estimate the relevant elasticities. These show the degree to which a given percentage change in the country's export receipts was associated with a change in the central government's revenues or expenditures.[33]

The Appendix to this chapter presents the econometric model that was used to answer these questions. The results show a very close correlation between the growth of Brazil's exports and the growth of central government revenues and expenditure. Moreover, because of the statistical techniques employed, the correlation results do *not* reflect the fact that all of these time series contain strong trends. Further, by the nature of the variables specified (exports and a current public-finance variable), the direction of first-order causality in this case is clear: from expanding foreign trade to the growth of central government fiscal resources. Finally, the parameters estimated also enable us to compute the long-run elasticities of central government expenditure and revenue with respect to exports. Both of these elasticities are close to unity. Thus the country's public finance expanded along a path which was almost completely parallel with Brazil's export expansion. As this finding indicates, the growth of state expenditures in Brazil through the nineteenth century was indeed constrained by the slow pace at which the country's foreign trade increased during most of the period.

Toward the end of the century, central government expenditures in Brazil showed a remarkable spurt. Between 1898 and 1913, government spending valued in constant sterling prices rose at a trend rate of 10 percent per annum.[34] To some extent, this extraordinary fiscal expansion reflects recovery from a cyclical trough. A shift in the tax base toward the industrial sector also played a role in the increase. But even as late as 1913, the share of industry in aggregate Brazilian output was too small to offer a major source of tax revenues. More importantly, the statistical results presented in the Appendix indicate that the steep rise in government spending which occurred in the last fifteen years of our period can be explained in part by the concomitant upsurge in Brazil's exports.[35] Finally, there were important political changes which facilitated relaxation of the public-finance constraint during these years (see below).

The sharp increase in government expenditure toward the end of the century had important consequences for Brazil's economic development. The acceleration in overall expenditure occurred conjointly with the shift in the pattern of government allocations. As noted earlier, these decades saw a decline in the share of government spending that was allocated for integrative functions, and a rise in the fraction that was spent for economic development. These two changes – the overall increase and the compositional shift – were multiplicative in terms of their impact on the magnitude of government investment in economic infrastructure. Together, they constituted an important non-linearity which spurred the development process in Brazil at the turn of the nineteenth century.

Constitutional Structure and Change

Thus far, our discussion of the low levels of central government expenditure during most of the century has focused largely on economic factors. Political conditions were obviously also important.[36] In particular, conditions related to political integration influenced the country's constitutional arrangements, and hence the capacity to mobilize tax revenues. Between 1834 and 1840, Brazil experimented with a decentralized ('federal') political system. However, serious centrifugal pressures emerged, and a tightly centralized constitutional structure was reinstituted. Throughout most of the nineteenth century, then, Brazil had a unitary rather than a federal political structure. Of special relevance here, control over economic-policy instruments was highly centralized in the unitary system, especially in matters of taxation and overseas borrowing.

This centralized political structure cannot be dismissed as an unimportant legal epiphenomenon, for the constitutional arrangements affected public finance and the level of aggregate development expenditure in two ways. First, Brazil's provincial governments were not able to take on the large public-investment role which the states filled in the United States.[37] Brazil's provincial and local governments were responsible for providing primary education. They were also legally empowered to make other promotional investments and subsidize private ventures. Under the prevailing constitutional structure, however, Brazil's provincial (and local) governments lacked the fiscal resources necessary to fulfill development responsibilities that involved large-scale expenditure. This deficiency was all the more serious because, as noted earlier, voluntary associations seem also to have played a relatively modest role in the supply of public goods in Brazil.

Second, the unitary constitutional structure may have limited the volume of public-finance resources that Brazil's socioeconomic elites were willing to accord to the *central* government. This hypothesis is suggested both on empirical and on theoretical grounds. Public-finance theory has emphasized that even under favorable conditions, the supply of public goods will probably be sub-optimal from a social viewpoint; for individual political participants are unlikely to reveal their true preferences concerning the supply of public goods. That standard problem was greatly exacerbated in this historical context, however, by conditions which stemmed from the centralized political structure. Because of their geographical dispersion, political participants in Brazil had very different preferences concerning the net benefits of potential public-sector investment projects which would be located in diverse provinces. Such location-specific preferences can be accommodated within a political system whose fiscal functions are decentralized.[38] However, with a unitary structure and multiple geographical participants – the situation that prevailed in Brazil during most of the century – the supply of public-goods is likely to be especially sub-optimal.

Further, theoretical considerations also indicate that in a decentralized system of representative democracy, the government is more likely to be responsive to the preferences of political participants.[39] By contrast, in a centralized structure, the state can achieve greater autonomy *vis-à-vis* other political actors. But since participants in a highly centralized structure can exert less control over the allocation of fiscal resources, they have less assurance that they (rather than other participants) will benefit from the way in which their taxes are used. Because of this uncertainty, political actors in a unitary structure will rationally accede to a lower level of taxation than will participants in a decentralized system. In the latter case, taxpayers have more control over allocational decisions and, consequently, greater certainty that their taxes will be spent in accordance with their own preferences.

These analytical perspectives are in fact supported by public-finance behavior in contemporary less-developed countries. With other conditions held constant, the share of total government taxation in GNP is lower in less-developed countries which have centralized rather than decentralized fiscal arrangements.[40] These empirical observations are consistent with our earlier theoretical discussion. Hence it seems plausible that volitional factors which were given scope by Brazil's constitutional structure constrained the size of central government revenues and expenditures during the nineteenth century. Brazil's fiscal experience during the Paraguayan War supports this interpretation. The war confronted Brazil's elites with the need for a classic public-good – national defense – which appeared to benefit all political participants. Table 5.3 presents information on central government spending and tax receipts before, during, and after the war years (1864–70).

Table 5.3 indicates that government revenues and expenditures rose sharply during the war years. Thus the war seems to have offered a generalized public good whose presence overcame the political impediments to public-finance supply which we discussed above. Table 5.3 also suggests another effect stemming from institutional conditions. The data show a distinct ratchet (or plateau) in Brazilian public finance. Government revenues followed the sharp rise in expenditures, and reached a much higher level in the war years. Moreover, this upward shift continued in the post-1870 period. This shift is evident in the behavior of the annual residuals of the central government revenue equation which is presented in the Appendix to this chapter.[41] Those residuals show that in fifteen of the twenty years following 1870, government receipts exceeded the level predicted by

Table 5.3   *Central Government Revenues and Expenditures before, during and after the Paraguayan War (in millions of* mil-réis)

Period	Average Annual Government Revenues	Average Annual Government Expenditures
1858–59 to 1860–61	46.9	52.6
1861–62 to 1863–64	51.9	55.5
1864–65 to 1866–67	*60.1*	*108.7*
1867–68 to 1869–70	*84.5*	*152.8*
1870–71 to 1872–73	103.0	107.8

Note: The annual data of Table 5.3 are presented in accordance with Brazil's fiscal year system. The figures in italics refer to wartime years.
Source: Computed from data in Oliver Ónody, *A Inflação Brasileira* (Rio de Janeiro, 1958), pp. 197–8.

that revenue-supply equation.[42] Thus once the Brazilian state increased its access (via the war) to public-finance resources, these gains were not completely reversible.

The preceding discussion has noted the importance of political and institutional conditions in nineteenth-century Brazil's public-finance constraint. That interpretation is also borne out by the subsequent course of events in Brazil. Following major constitutional changes in 1889, the country shifted from the centralized imperial regime, which we have discussed, to a federal Republic. This shift involved more than a change in façade, for it led to two changes which are important in the present context. First, the new constitutional structure decentralized power and functions, and gave the states far greater autonomy in fiscal affairs and overseas borrowing. Some state (and local) governments responded energetically to the opportunities offered by the new arrangements; and a larger total volume of promotional activity and public-sector investment seems to have resulted.[43] Federalism led to both a rise in the taxes levied by some states and a major increase in state and municipal overseas borrowing, largely for infrastructure investment.[44] Between 1888 and 1915, the external debt of Brazil's overall public sector rose from £33 million to £172 million. State and local borrowing accounted for fully 42 percent of this large increment.[45] Similarly, the 1906 program for coffee valorization was largely the effort of the major coffee-producing states, and might not have been feasible under the earlier centralized structure.[46]

Of equal importance were the new constitution's 'republican' aspects. These, too, facilitated greater responsiveness on the part of the central government to private-sector interests. The new structure featured election of the chief of state by Brazil's socioeconomic elites – a change from the previous system of hereditary succession. In addition, the chief executive no longer had lifetime incumbency, as under the empire. Private-sector elites gained on both counts. Not only could they now exert more power in the initial selection of the chief executive, but they also had the enhanced influence which came with recurring elections.[47]

The greater sensitivity to private-sector interests under the new constitutional structure seems to have facilitated a number of promotional policy efforts in subsequent decades. We have already noted the rising share of capital formation in total central government expenditure during this period. In particular, partly as a result of subsidy and investment programs implemented by the central government and by the states, railroad construction accelerated sharply. In 1889, Brazil had approximately 9,600 kilometers of railway trackage; by 1913, the figure was 24,600.[48] Other governmental actions that were believed to be developmental were also instituted under the new regime: for example, increased tariff protection for industry and for the domestic agricultural sector, and the measures which led to the credit expansion and stock exchange boom of the early 1890s (the '*encilhamento*'). Finally, the enhanced political control which the republican constitution gave to Brazil's socioeconomic elites may also have helped the central government play a more effective public-finance role. With greater certainty that their taxes would be used for the purposes they preferred, private-sector interests may have been more willing to accord the government the resources which relaxed the public-finance constraint. These conditions probably contributed to the sharp acceleration in real central government expenditure which we noted for the post-1898 years.

The foregoing discussion suggests that it may not have been pure coincidence that the onset of sustained economic development in Brazil followed the shift from the imperial regime to the Republic. The dangers of *post hoc ergo propter hoc* reasoning are evident. However, we have also proposed the necessary causal connections: a relaxation of the public-finance constraint, and the increased responsiveness of the government to private-sector economic interests. Both of these changes were accelerated with the advent of the decentralized and republican constitutional structure.

An important question remains unanswered. The changes in Brazil's constitutional structure cannot be considered as independent of underlying political and economic forces. What was the direction of causation in the process that led to formation of a more rational structure linking the political system and the economy? The purely political tensions which preceded the constitutional change were considerable. Consequently, one may be tempted to posit the primacy of the political. But important economic changes were also occurring in Brazil at this time.[49] Mutually-reinforcing causation between economic and political forces is of course another plausible hypothesis. The direction(s) of causality here remains to be clarified.

Conclusions

The Brazilian government during the nineteenth century was relatively effective in holding the country together, and maintaining social and political stability. Government policy was also successful in maintaining an elastic supply of low-cost labor from overseas. This was an orientation which had important implications for the returns to land and capital, and for the distribution of income in nineteenth-century Brazil.

During most of the century, however, the Brazilian state was much less effective in the area of infrastructure investment. Until the end of the period, the government failed to promote large-scale investment in social overhead capital, and particularly in the construction of facilities (such as railroads) which would have lowered transportation costs in Brazil's interior. Public action here was especially important because private returns in infrastructure investment were apparently so low in many cases that such facilities had to be supplied (or subsidized) by the state if they were to be provided at all. Nevertheless, until the end of the century, the government failed to provide the country with social overhead capital on a scale large enough to permit rapid economic development.

Two hypotheses present themselves as likely explanations for the limited supply of public goods in nineteenth-century Brazil: excessive deference to *laissez-faire* doctrines, and the pressures of vested interests. As we have seen, however, neither of these explanations can account for the failure of public policy in this instance. Rather, a large-scale public investment program seems to have been impeded by the meager fiscal resources which Brazil's socioeconomic elites and state allocated for development purposes during most of the century. The public-finance constraint reduced both the size of the government's own investment activities and the scale of the subsidy program which it could offer private investors.

Three sets of conditions, in turn, explain the initial severity and the subsequent relaxation of the constraint on government development expenditure. As we have seen, the state's major source of tax revenues in nineteenth-century Brazil was the country's foreign-trade sector. This heavy reliance on foreign-trade duties seriously limited the size of the country's public finances, for until the end of the century, Brazil's exports and imports were too small to provide substantial government revenues. Second, the state initially allocated most of its aggregate spending to the principal instruments of political integration, the bureaucracy and the military. It was only toward the end of the period that the share of economic development in central government expenditure rose to higher levels.

Finally, as part of its effort to maintain the country's territorial integrity, the state maintained a unitary political system rather than one in which power was effectively decentralized. In particular, public-finance decisions were very much under the control of the central government. This constitutional structure seems to have reduced the total supply of public-goods in nineteenth-century Brazil. Not only were the provincial and local governments constrained in their capacity to mobilize fiscal resources, but the system may also have limited the volume of the public finance which Brazil's socioeconomic elites were willing to accord to the state. Brazil's shift, after 1889, to a federal and republican structure involved a major change in this context. In addition to the increase scope for initiative at the provincial level, the constitutional change enhanced government responsiveness to private-sector pressures for developmental measures.

These explanations – the size of the country's foreign trade and the effective tax base, the government's allocational pattern, and the effects of constitutional structure in distorting or facilitating political responsiveness – should obviously be regarded as complements rather than alternatives. Their credibility may be enhanced by the fact that they explain *both* the initial low levels of government development expenditure and the subsequent easing of the public-finance constraint toward the end of the nineteenth century.

Brazil's experience during the nineteenth century also suggests some conclusions of broader relevance. One implication is clear – the supply of fiscal resources can be of strategic importance for economic development. Brazil's political elite learned this lesson well. They subsequently established a fiscal system that was to give the public sector a relatively large share in the country's national income.[50] Another conclusion concerns the importance of institutions in the development process. Conditions stemming from Brazil's political sociology led first to the formation of a unitary political structure, and subsequently to a more decentralized regime. As we have seen, such institutional arrangements had important side-effects, first exacerbating and later relaxing the public-finance constraint on the country's economic development. This experience suggests that institutions can be more than a façade for political-sociology conditions. In this instance, institutional structure had independent effects in transmitting (and in some ways distorting) the political preferences of socioeconomic elites.

Finally, this chapter also suggests a tentative answer for the case of Brazil to the classic question of the relation, if any, between representative government and economic development. For the reasons discussed, nineteenth-century Brazil might well have experienced sustained economic development earlier and at a higher rate if the country had been governed by a more responsive regime.[51]

Appendix: The Growth of Exports and the Growth of Central Government Revenues and Expenditures in Nineteenth-Century Brazil

As discussed in the text of this chapter, in the nineteenth century Brazil's central government seems to have operated under a public-finance constraint determined by the supply of fiscal resources. And because of the conditions we have considered, exports constituted the Brazilian state's principal tax base during most of the century. This Appendix tests these propositions with historical data. We also estimate the elasticities of government revenue and expenditure with respect to the country's exports.

These elasticities might in principle be estimated by regressing annual observations of the logarithm of, say, government revenues, R, against annual observations of the logarithm of Brazilian exports, X. Such a procedure, however, would probably involve specification error. It is unlikely that government tax revenues adjusted completely to a change in X within one year; consequently, the long-run elasticity of R with respect to a change in X may well differ from the short-run response. Because of the possibility of such a distributed-lag response, we will utilize a partial-adjustment model.[52] The equations to be estimated are therefore of the form:

$$\ln R = a\lambda + b \ln X + (1-\lambda) \ln R_{-1} + u, \tag{1}$$

where b is an estimate of the short-run elasticity; λ measures the speed with which actual R adjusts to equilibrium R; $(1-\lambda)/\lambda$ is the mean adjustment lag; b/λ is the estimated long-run elasticity of R with respect to X; and u is the error term.

Before proceeding to estimate equations with this specification for R and G (government expenditure), we must note another potential pitfall. The series for G, R, and X, are characterized by strong time trends. Consequently, estimation of equation (1) might yield spuriously good fits which would reflect nothing more than serial correlation in the error term. To guard against this possibility, statistical tests were performed on the estimates of u in the equations with G and R as the dependent variables.[53] The results of these tests indicated that ordinary least-squares estimation (OLS) does not lead to inefficient estimates in the equation for G. In the equation for R, however, OLS is not appropriate. Accordingly, the Hildreth-Liu procedure was utilized to estimate the serial correlation parameter ρ.

For the years 1823–1913, we observe the following results for the R equation (absolute values of t-ratios are in parentheses):

$$\ln R = -.299 + .315 \ln X + .707 \ln R_{-1} \tag{1a}$$
$$\quad\ (3.28)(5.01) \qquad (12.22)$$

$$R^2 = .99 \qquad \rho = .250 \ (2.44)$$

$$b = .315 \qquad \lambda = .293 \qquad (1-\lambda)/\lambda = 2.41 \qquad b/\lambda = 1.08$$

All the parameters of equation (1a) are highly significant, and the equation tracks the growth of central government revenues very well. Of greater analytical interest, the parameter estimates provide important information concerning Brazil's fiscal system during the nineteenth century. The parameter estimate for ρ, the serial-correlation coefficient, indicates a somewhat sluggish response of government revenues to current economic changes. Similarly, the mean adjustment to equilibrium values of R occurred only after 2.4 years. The short-run elasticity of R with respect to X is .315; that is, a 10 percent change in export receipts was associated with a movement of some 3.2 percent in government revenues during the same year. The long-run elasticity, however, was much higher, 1.08. Thus export growth led to a slightly more-than-proportional increase in government revenues.

The estimates for the government-expenditure equation are:

$$\ln G = -.240 + .368 \ln X + .645 \ln G_{-1} \qquad (1b)$$
$$(2.37)\,(4.80) \qquad (9.09)$$

$$R^2 = .98$$

$$b = .368 \qquad \lambda = .355 \qquad (1-\lambda)/\lambda = 1.82 \qquad b/\lambda = 1.04$$

The parameter estimate for b in equation (1b) shows that in the short run, a 10 percent increase in Brazil's export receipts was associated with a 3.7 percent increase in government spending. Thus the short-run response of G to a change in exports was slightly higher than for R. The adjustment to long-run equilibrium values was also somewhat faster, 1.8 years. These differences in the coefficients of the expenditure and revenue equations were reflected in Brazil's frequent budget deficits. Finally, and most importantly in the present context, the long-run elasticity of G with respect to changes in X was 1.04. This elasticity shows that government spending rose along a path almost completely parallel with the long-term increase in the country's exports.

Notes

1   There are of course many ways of conceptualizing the role of government in economic development, for the subject has been much discussed by philosophers as well as by social scientists from different disciplines. For a collection of thoughtful papers which analyzes the experience of several very diverse countries, see Hugh G. J. Aitken (ed.), *The State and Economic Growth* (New York: Social Science Research Council, 1959).

2   Concerning the influence of the large landowners early in the century, see, for example, Alan K. Manchester, 'The Rise of the Brazilian Aristocracy,' *Hispanic American Historical Review*, vol. 11 (May 1931). Concerning class and pressure-group political activity, see also Eugene W. Ridings, 'Class Sector Unity in an Export Economy: The Case of Nineteenth-Century Brazil,' *Hispanic American Historial Review*, vol. 58, no. 3 1978; and for the last decades of our period, Steven Topkin, 'The Evolution of The Economic Role of The Brazilian State 1889–1930,' *Journal of Latin American Studies*, vol. 11 (March 1979). For a discussion of the general issues involved in political model-building for nineteenth-century Brazil, see Richard Graham, 'Political Power and Land-ownership in Nineteenth-Century Latin America,' in Richard Graham and Peter Smith (eds.), *New Approaches to Latin American History* (Austin: University of Texas Press, 1974), pp. 112–36.

3   See the classic study of Raymondo Faoro, *Os Donos Do Poder*, 2nd edn (São Paulo, 1975). Different scholars have tended to emphasize different sides of the same coin. Thus some historians have given prominence to the power of the country's political-bureaucratic elite, and others have stressed the political influence of the export sector. The extent and limits of symbiosis between these two groups do not seem to have been adequately explored. On the usefulness of some of the analytical models which are often applied to Latin American politics during this period, see the critical discussion in Frank Stafford, 'Bases of Political Alignment in Early Spanish America,' in Graham and Smith (eds.), *New Approaches*, op. cit., pp. 71–112.

4   For example, on the effects of political instability in impeding the economic development of Mexico during the nineteenth century, see Henry C. Aubrey, 'Deliberate Industrialization,' *Social Research* (August 1949).

5   See Chapter 2, pp. 25–30, above.

6   Peter Smith, 'Political Legitimacy in Spanish America,' in Graham and Smith (eds.), *New Approaches*, op. cit., p. 247.

7   See Kenneth R. Maxwell, 'The Generation of the 1790's and The Idea of Luso-Brazilian Empire,' in Dauril Alden (ed.), *Colonial Roots of Modern Brazil* (Baltimore: Johns Hopkins University Press, 1975), pp. 107–44. By contrast, Spain followed a different course in relation to its South American colonies. This led to military and ideological mobilization, which set the stage for a post-independence political pattern very different from Brazil's.

8   See E. S. Pang and R. L. Seckinger, 'The Mandarins of Imperial Brazil,' *Comparative Studies in Society and History*, vol. 14 (March 1972); and José Murilo de Carvalho, 'Elite and State-Building in Imperial Brazil' (PhD dissertation, Stanford University, 1974).

9   On these points, see Nathaniel H. Leff, *Underdevelopment and Development in Brazil*, Vol. I *Economic Structure and Change*, (London: Allen & Unwin, 1982), Chapters 6 and 7.

10 See Leff, *Economic Structure and Change*, op. cit., Chapter 8.

11 A. P. Lerner, 'The Symmetry between Import and Export Taxes,' *Economica*, vol. 3 (August 1936); and R. I. McKinnon, 'Intermediate Products and Differential Tariffs: A Generalization of Lerner's Symmetry Theorem,' *Quarterly Journal of Economics* 81 (November 1966).

12 On the ideological pattern which was more common in Latin America in the nineteenth century, see Albert O. Hirschman, 'Ideologies of Economic Development in Latin America,' in Albert O. Hirschman (ed.), *Latin American Issues* (New York: Twentieth Century Fund, 1961), esp. pp. 8–9.

13 For a more extended discussion of the phenomena which are mentioned in the preceding paragraph, see Leff, *Economic Structure and Change*, op. cit., Chapter 4, pp. 48–67.

14 The terms 'public-goods' and 'external economies' are used in their technical sense, following standard usage in the theory of public finance. For an exposition see, for example, Peter O. Steiner 'Public Expenditure Budgeting,' in Alan Blinder *et al.*, *The Economics of Public Finance* (Washington: The Brookings Institution, 1974), esp. pp. 243–56.

15 The background material for the points mentioned in this paragraph is presented in Leff, *Economic Structure and Change*, op. cit., Chapters 2 and 7. The discussion here deals mainly with government promotion of investment in transportation facilities such as railways. Some aspects of the situation with respect to investment in education are discussed in Leff, ibid., Chapter 2.

16 Joseph A. Schumpeter, *Capitalism, Socialism, and Democracy*, (New York: Harper, 1942). For a corroboration (in a contemporary underdeveloped country) of the approach suggested in the text, see J. M. Guttman, 'Villages as Interest Groups: The Demand for Agricultural Extension Services in India,' *Kyklos*, vol. 33, no. 1 (1980), esp. pp. 124–7.

17 Mancur Olson, Jr, *The Logic of Collective Action: Public Goods and the Theory of Groups*, (Cambridge, Mass.: Harvard University Press, 1965), pp. 22–36, 43–65.

18 On these points, see Leff, *Economic Structure and Change*, Chapters 6 and 7. The elastic supply of labor in nineteenth-century Brazil is documented in ibid., Chapter 4.

19 This figure was computed from data in a compilation that was prepared for Philippe Schmitter's and John Coatsworth's 1977 Workshop in 'Historical Perspectives on the State, Society, and Economy in Latin America' (mimeo., University of Chicago, 1977), p. 17.

20 Data available for 1856 indicate that local governments accounted for approximately 3 percent of total public-sector expenditures (the latter defined as the sum of the expenditures by the central government, the provincial governments, and the

municípios). In 1885–86, the proportion was 5 percent. These figures are from José Murilo de Carvalho, 'Elite and State-Building,' op. cit., p. 310.

21   See Leff, *Economic Structure and Change*, Chapter 2.

22   The Brazilian state may of course have spent more on the military and on the bureaucracy than was necessary to achieve its integrative goals. Note further that international comparisons are of little help in making judgments on this point. For example, military personnel amounted to some .3 percent of Brazil's total population in 1876, and .2 percent in 1889. The corresponding figures for the United States were .1 percent in 1871, and .06 percent in 1891. (These data are from José Murilo de Carvalho, 'Elite and State-Building,' op. cit., pp. 389–90.) By contrast, the average figure for a sample of eighteen European states in 1858 was 1 percent – much higher than the ratio for Brazil. (The European figure is from Frederic Pryor, *Public Expenditures in Communist and Capitalist Nations* (Homewood, Ill.: R. D. Irwin, 1968), pp. 101–2.) Such international comparisons, however, cannot provide a basis for inferences concerning the efficiency of public-sector expenditure. Additional information concerning 'objective' security needs, elite preferences, and relative factor costs is also needed to distinguish the separate influences on allocational patterns in specific cases.

23   Bert F. Hoselitz, 'Economic Policy and Economic Development,' in Aitken (ed.), *The State and Economic Growth*, op. cit., esp. pp. 333–4, 339.

24   Computed from data in Annibal Villela and Wilson Suzigan, *Política do Governo e Crescimento da Economia Brasileira, 1889–1945* (Rio de Janeiro: IPEA, 1973), p. 414. Note that the 'economic development' category of Table 5.2 differs from the 'fixed capital formation' of the source just cited. The former category includes items such as expenditure on public education and railroad subsidies.

25   Richard A. Musgrave, *Fiscal Systems* (New Haven: Yale University Press, 1969), pp. 118–19; J. R. Lotz and E. R. Morss 'A Theory of Tax Level Determinants in Developing Countries,' *Economic Development and Cultural Change*, vol. 18 (April 1970). Brazil's fiscal heterodoxy led to frequent budget deficits: hence, annual government expenditures were not constrained to equal annual receipts. Nevertheless, expenditures could not be totally unrelated to revenues because of the inflationary and balance-of-payments consequences of complete de-coupling. Consequently, the level of tax revenues also affected government expenditure levels.

26   See pp. 84–5 in Chapter 4, above.

27   Richard Bird, *Taxing Agricultural Land in Developing Countries* (Cambridge, Mass.: Harvard University Press, 1974), Chapter 5, and 'Land Taxation and Economic Development: The Model of Meiji Japan,' *Journal of Development Studies*, vol. 23 (January 1977), esp. Table 1.

28   Evsey Domar, 'The Causes of Slavery or Serfdom: A Hypotheses,' *Journal of Economic History*, vol. 30 (March 1970).

29   On these points, see Leff, *Economic Structure and Change*, op. cit., Chapter 5, pp. 80–1.

30   These figures were completed from data in Mircea Buescu, *300 Anos de Inflação* (Rio de Janeiro: APEC, 1973), p. 201. Buescu's data, in turn, are from Amaro Cavalcanti. If money issued by the government is included in the debt, the per capita figure for 1864 was £2.4; and for 1870, £5.5.

31   Computed from data in José Murilo de Carvalho, 'Elite and State Building,' op. cit., pp. 570, 580–1.

32   As discussed in Leff, *Economic Structure and Change*, op. cit., Chapter 6, the overall rate of price increase in Brazil was probably in the neighborhood of 2.5 percent per annum during this period. That discussion also indicates that Brazil's internal rate of price inflation, including products of the domestic agricultural sector, exceeded the pace at which the country's exchange rate depreciated. Consequently, the domestic purchasing power of government rose by much less than is implied by the sterling values presented in Table 5.1, above.

33 Brazil's provincial governments also levied some foreign-trade duties. This hardly invalidates the present analysis, however, for the bulk of the country's foreign-trade taxes went to the central government. Moreover, as indicated in the text, export receipts are also interpreted here as a proxy for the size of the public-finance base in the economy's advanced sector.

34 The *t*-value for this trend coefficient is 10.5. The trend regression was computed using the data on the annual sterling value of central government expenditure. The deflator used to compute the series in constant (1880) sterling prices is the export price series of Great Britain. That series was taken from Albert H. Imlah, *Economic Elements in the Pax Britannica* (Cambridge, Mass.: Harvard University Press, 1958), pp. 94–8. During the preceding two decades, from 1878 to 1897, the value of central government expenditure in constant sterling prices had risen at a trend rate of only 2.1 percent per annum.

35 See also Leff, *Economic Structure and Change*, op. cit., Chapter 5, Table 5.1.

36 The discussion here focuses on questions which are familiar from classical political philosophy: the constitutional arrangements which are best suited for providing socially desirable governmental decisions. The mode of analysis, however, is closer to what Paul Samuelson has called 'welfare politics'. See his paper 'The Pure Theory of Public Expenditure,' *Review of Economics and Statistics*, vol. 36 (November 1954), p. 389.

37 See, for example, Henry W. Broude, 'The Role of the State in American Economic Development, 1820–1890,' in Aitken (ed.), *The State and Economic Growth*, op. cit., p. 12; Carter Goodrich, *Government Promotion of American Canals and Railroads, 1800–1890* (New York: Columbia University Press, 1959).

38 John G. Head, 'Public Goods and Multi-Level Government,' in W. L. David (ed.), *Public Finance, Planning, and Economic Development* (New York: St. Martin's Press, 1973), esp. p. 25.

39 Albert Breton, *The Economic Theory of Representative Government* (Chicago: University of Chicago Press, 1974), pp. 44–8, 113–16, 156, n. The political participants in nineteenth-century Brazil's 'representative democracy' were of course only the upper classes.

40 Lotz and Morss, 'Tax Level Determinants in Developing Countries,' op. cit., pp. 334–338. As Lotz and Morss emphasize (p. 338, n.) this finding holds only for less-developed countries. See also the statistical results reported by Pryor, *Public Expenditure*, op. cit., pp. 438–40; and Wallace Oates, *Fiscal Federalism* (New York: Harcourt, Brace, and Jovanovich, 1972), pp. 210–11, 219. The difference in statistical results as between samples of more and less-developed countries presumably reflects differences in political integration and in ease of access to tax bases.

41 The residuals are the annual differences between the actual and the fitted values of the equation. The equation cited in the text is equation (1b) of the Appendix.

42 Note that the effect of war on Brazilian public finance gives some support to the 'displacement effect' theory of wars on public finance. See Alan Peacock and Jack Wiseman, *The Growth of Public Expenditure in the United Kingdom* (Princeton University Press, 1961), pp. 24.

43 Celso Furtado has also noted aspects of the post-1889 regime's decentralization and its impact on subsequent economic development. See his *Formação Econômica do Brasil*, 5th edn (Rio de Janeiro: Fundo de Cultura, 1963), Chapter 29, pp. 200–1.

44 See, for example, John Wirth, *Minas Gerais in the Brazilian Federation, 1889–1937* (Stanford: Stanford University Press, 1977), pp. 262–5.

45 These figures were computed from data which are presented in 'Historical Perspectives on the State, Society, and Economy in Latin America,' op. cit., pp. 15–16.

46 Note, however, that the new constitution's decentralized structure did not enable the Northeast to break out of its regional decline. See the discussion in Chapter 2, pp. 29–30, above.

47 Breton, *The Economic Theory of Representative Democracy*, op. cit., pp. 48–9.

Note, however, that even under the imperial regime, socioeconomic elites had some influence (through parliamentary elections) on the appointment of the President of the Council of Ministers.

48 'Historical Perspectives,' op. cit., p. 22.

49 See Leff, *Economic Structure and Change*, op. cit., Chapter 7, pp. 146–61 and Chapter 6, pp. 117–20.

50 Dennis J. Mahar and Fernando A. Rezende, 'The Growth of Public Expenditure in Brazil, 1920–1969,' *Public Finance Quarterly*, vol. 3 (October 1975); R. J. Chelliah, 'Trends in Taxation in Developing Countries,' *IMF Staff Papers* (July 1971).

51 In the first decades of the post-Second World War period, there was also no empirical basis for a statistical expectation that less-developed countries with authoritarian regimes experience higher rates of economic development than more responsive regimes. See the data presented in G. Dick, 'Authoritarian vs. Non-Authoritarian Approaches to Economic Development,' *Journal of Political Economy*, vol. 82 (August 1974).

52 In formal terms, the model utilized here resembles the partial-adjustment model which is presented in the Appendix to Chapter 3, above. For a full exposition of this model, see Marc Nerlove, *The Dynamics of Supply: Estimation of Farmers' Response to Price* (Baltimore: Johns Hopkins University Press, 1958). In his survey of such models ('Distributed Lags: A Survey,' *Econometrica*, vol. 35), Zvi Griliches has emphasized that researchers must also ascertain that the model they are estimating is indeed characterized by a partial-adjustment process rather than simply one of serial correlation. In the econometric work reported below, I used the statistical test which Griliches proposed; and the results indicated that a partial-adjustment is appropriate for the equations presented.

53 For a general discussion of the econometric questions raised here and for a description of the Hildreth-Liu correction procedure, see, for example, Robert Pindyck and Daniel Rubinfeld, *Econometric Models and Economic Forecasts* (New York: McGraw-Hill, 1976), pp. 106–12. The statistical test used to determine the presence of serial correlation in the distributed-lag estimates is described in P. Dhrymes, *Distributed Lags* (San Francisco: Holden-Day, 1971), pp. 350–1.

6
Conclusions

Looking Backward

This book has analyzed the conditions which underlay the two major features of Brazil's economic experience in the nineteenth century. During most of the century, Brazil failed to achieve a high rate of economic development. Because of its cumulative effects, this experience had important consequences for the level of economic well-being in Brazil both during and after the nineteenth century. And because the United States and some countries in Western Europe were achieving sustained economic progress during the period, Brazil's poor economic performance helped make Brazil an economically backward country. Brazil's modest development during the nineteenth century takes on special analytical interest because of the sequel to that experience – the country's long period of slow development was followed by the onset of rapid economic growth and long-term structural change. These began in Brazil toward the end of the nineteenth century.

Part of Brazil's slow overall development during the nineteenth century can be attributed to conditions in the Northeast. Almost half of the country's population resided in that region, and suffered from its particularly poor economic experience. The proximate cause of the Northeast's unhappy experience was the unsatisfactory performance of its sugar and cotton exports. Chapter 2 discussed the supply and demand conditions which these commodities faced. As we saw there, a major factor in the Northeast's plight was the fact that it was part of the same political and economic unit as Brazil's Southeast. The Northeast's prime products were not the commodities which were favored for export under Brazilian comparative advantage. In addition, since the Northeast was part of the larger nation state, exchange-rate adjustment was precluded as a means for achieving higher export growth and development. Worse still, as a part of the larger political and economic unit, the Northeast's problems were actually aggravated by the unitary exchange-rate mechanism.

More generally, widespread economic development in Brazil required important changes in the conditions affecting the country's domestic agricultural sector.[1] A large fraction of the country's labor force was engaged in this sector, but its productivity growth suffered from the absence of low-cost transportation within Brazil's interior. Facing heavy (and in many cases prohibitive) freight charges for their high bulk/low value commodities, producers in the domestic agricultural sector could not benefit fully from the gains to market integration and intraregional specialization. In addition, high transportation costs made for steep price–distance gradients in the supply of foodstuffs. Consequently, growth in Brazil's 'advanced' sector of export and urban activities was slowed by an inelastic supply of wage goods.

Internal transportation costs were high in Brazil because of unfavorable geographical conditions. The country's natural waterways were not well situated from an economic point of view. And individual waterways within the better endowed regions did not interconnect in a manner similar to the Missouri–Mississippi or the Great Lakes systems in the United States. Under these conditions, sustained development in Brazil had to await the provision of man-made infrastructure facilities such as roads or railways. Such transportation facilities were necessary to shift domestic agricultural supply curves downward, and increase their elasticity. Those changes, in turn, were essential if Brazil was to have more generalized economic growth and more favorable intersectoral linkages.

Unfortunately, the stock of infrastructure facilities increased very slowly in nineteenth-century Brazil. Externalities and collective-good aspects were often involved in the provision of roads and railways; consequently, public finance for subsidies or government investment was usually necessary. But through most of the nineteenth century, conditions in Brazil's public sector were not propitious for a large-scale investment or promotional effort in social overhead capital. Ideological rigidities were not the problem here.[2] Nor did the difficulties stem from the fact that large landowners had great influence in Brazilian politics.]On the contrary,]oligarchical rule *per se* might have been expected to increase public-sector investment in infrastructure.[3] Other conditions, however, acted to impose a severe public-finance constraint on the supply of public investment in nineteenth-century Brazil.

As we saw in Chapter 5, Brazil's governments experienced considerable difficulty in mobilizing fiscal resources during the nineteenth century. Tax revenues were drawn mainly from the country's external sector. But for most of the period, Brazil's exports were not very large; hence, the size of the principal tax base was small. By contrast, revenues derived from Brazil's domestic sector were relatively minor. This feature of Brazil's fiscal system reflected the country's factor endowment. With the abundant land available in nineteenth-century Brazil, cultivation in the domestic agricultural sector was land-extensive and production was characterized by high land–labor ratios. Consequently Ricardian rent, which might have provided the basis for agricultural taxation, was small. Further, with poor communications and high illiteracy rates in the interior, the transactions costs of taxing the domestic agricultural sector were high.

Other conditions associated with Brazil's endowment of land (and space) also contributed to the public-finance constraint on development expenditure. Geographically, Brazil is a vast country. Moreover, under the transportation conditions prevailing in the nineteenth century, distances in economic terms were especially large. Further, the country's natural resources were distributed unevenly across space; hence distinct regions (and sub-regions) emerged. And given the political and economic conditions which characterized Brazil in the nineteenth century – not least, poor communications – there were strong centrifugal forces and a real threat of territorial fragmentation.

Reacting to this situation, Brazil's political elites maintained a unitary and highly centralized state for most of the century. What is important in the present context is that these arrangements included a tight fiscal centralization, with only modest revenue sources left to the provincial and local governments. This fiscal system did not encourage a large flow of resources for 'public improvements' at the sub-national level. Further, the conjunction of a unitary state in a country of vast territory and distinct regions may also have reduced the supply of public finance in another way. Many infrastructure projects (e.g. for transportation purposes) were by their nature location-specific. The major revenue bases, however, were allocated for taxes which went to the central government. As a result, landowners in Brazil faced considerable uncertainty as to whether the taxes which they might pay at the national level would be spent for investment projects from which they, in their own locales, would benefit.

Finally, the geographical and political conditions we have discussed affected the expenditure (as well as the revenue) side of Brazil's public finances. Faced with the danger of political fragmentation, the country's elites gave their highest priority to government spending for integrative purposes. Consequently, the military and administrative apparatus had first claim on government spending. And given the meager total of overall fiscal resources in Brazil for most of the nineteenth century, the amounts left over for economic development were modest. It was only in the last decades of the period that the level of government expenditure for integrative functions stabilized, and the share of spending for economic development increased rapidly.

That change coincided with other shifts which also enlarged the total amount of investment in social overhead capital. Both government spending and foreign investment in Brazilian infrastructure projects accelerated in the last decades of the nineteenth century. The growth of Brazil's international trade was an important variable in this process; for expanding exports enlarged each of these sources of infrastructure capital. First, the flow of foreign investment to Brazil was partly a function of the country's export receipts. These affected the country's capacity to service foreign-capital payments. In addition, positive relations between export growth and the returns to foreign capital, and between the returns to foreign capital and the flow of new investment led to the same result. What is pertinent here is that in the last decades of the nineteenth century the size of Brazil's foreign trade sector increased considerably. Not surprisingly, the stock of foreign investment in the country's infrastructure facilities also rose sharply.[4]

Export growth also increased the capacity of Brazil's government to invest in social overhead capital. As mentioned earlier, the Brazilian state's revenues depended heavily on foreign-trade taxes. Government spending for development also rose because of changes internal to Brazil's public sector. As the share of government spending allocated to the military and the civil service fell, the share spent on social-overhead capital increased markedly. This compositional change meant that the fiscal resources available for developmental expenditure expanded much more than proportionately with total central government spending. Finally, in 1889 Brazil shifted to a republican and more decentralized regime. For the reasons discussed in Chapter 5, those changes, too, added to the tax revenues and the foreign-borrowing capacity of the aggregate public sector.

These changes in Brazil's public finances and foreign investment were additive. Together, they generated a sharp rise in the country's stock of social-overhead capital, particularly in railroads. As a result, sustained economic development began in Brazil, at least in the Southeast, where these changes were concentrated.

Our discussion of Brazil's experience also led to other conclusions concerning the barriers to economic progress in this historical case. Some hypotheses which may be appealing in *a priori* terms do not appear to be empirically relevant in explaining the country's slow economic development during the nineteenth century. And by the same token, the onset of rapid economic growth and structural change in Brazil does not seem to have been caused by shifts of some often-cited obstacles to development. For example, the materials presented in Chapter 3 do not support the view that sociocultural conditions were a major barrier to Brazil's economic progress during this period. Similarly, there are no indications that changes in the country's sociocultural conditions triggered Brazil's transition to sustained development.

Serious reservations also apply to an interpretation which attributes Brazil's limited development during the nineteenth century to international imperialism. As we have seen, the political, ideological, and economic relations that were fostered by Brazil's involvement in the international economy do not explain the country's failure to develop more rapidly.[5] More accurately, rising exports actually promoted Brazil's economic development.[6] Note further that the positive effects of export growth in Brazil went well beyond the impact within the external sector. The forward and backward linkages engendered by trade expansion stimulated higher output levels and real income growth in the domestic agricultural sector. Growing exports also helped promote Brazilian industrialization. And because of the impact of export growth on railroad construction, expanding exports led to an increase in internal trade and an intensification of intersectoral multiplier effects within Brazil.

Finally, the circumstances in which Brazil began its modern economic development also fail to support a dependency hypothesis. If anything, the contrary interpretation appears to be more accurate in this case. More widespread development in the Brazilian economy required increased elasticity of supply and higher output growth in the domestic agricultural sector. Those changes, in turn, depended on an enlargement of the country's stock of social-overhead capital. In practice, the resources for such infrastructure expansion in nineteenth-century Brazil came largely from two sources: foreign investment and the Brazilian state. Both of these instrumentalities grew in function of the country's foreign trade. Hence the flow of investment which helped develop the domestic agricultural sector depended directly on the size of the export sector. Under these conditions, it seems analytically unhelpful to view Brazil's export growth and increasing involvement in the international economy as retarding the country's development.

Analytical Reprise

It is also useful to discuss in more general terms the process and limits within which economic change occurred in nineteenth-century Brazil. Economic change took place here largely in response to movements in relative prices and rates of return. An analysis in these terms explains much of the development that occurred – and did not occur – in Brazil during the nineteenth century. In addition, this economic process was very much conditioned by the context within which it took place. One major set of contextual features involved the country's land endowment and geographical conditions. These raised internal transportation costs to a point where the scope for market transactions was often limited. Indeed, in the case of the Northeast, economic conditions which derived from geography precluded satisfactory market adjustment.[7]

The initial conditions which prevailed in Brazil at the start of the nineteenth century also influenced the country's subsequent development. Brazil began the period as a country that was characterized by some basic economic features: a low level of per capita productivity, a large fraction of slaves in the population, and a highly unequal distribution of income. These conditions combined to affect the distribution of political power, and hence the policy options that were effectively available for dealing with the country's economic problems. In particular, the privileged position of the large landowners in this system led to measures which maintained the country's elastic supply of low-cost labor from abroad. To preserve the pattern of wages and income distribution, the Brazilian government tenaciously resisted British pressure to stop the importation of slaves. After half a century Brazil was forced to capitulate, and slavery was ultimately abolished. The country's major economic and social features persisted, however, as Brazil's governments instituted programs to subsidize immigration from Europe and continue the elastic flow of labor from overseas. These measures to maintain large-scale importation of workers to Brazil can be interpreted as the market-*cum*-institutional response to the country's initial factor endowment of high land/labor ratios.[8] And partly because Brazil began the nineteenth century with lower income levels than the United States, the economic consequences of the population in-movements were also very different in the two countries.[9]

In addition to history and geography, conditions in other analytical domains also shaped Brazil's economic experience during the nineteenth century. The country's politics were of paramount importance. Moreover, the impact of politics on Brazil's economic history far transcended the often-cited fact of domination by a landowner oligarchy. The consequences which followed from the absence of political and fiscal decentralization were crucial; for they helped tighten the public-finance constraint on the country's development. Finally, Brazil's demographic conditions were another important feature of the overall context. The country's rate of aggregate population growth during the nineteenth century was relatively high: 1.6 percent per annum between 1822 and 1873; and 2.1 percent per annum between 1874 and 1913. This was only partly the result of labor importation. Natural demographic increase accounted for a large (and growing) fraction of Brazil's total population growth during the nineteenth century.[10] This high rate of internal demographic increase had two important consequences. First, it determined a pace of labor-force growth in the domestic agricultural sector which was high compared to the growth of productivity in the sector. The high rate of natural increase also made for a relatively young age-structure in Brazil's population. Coming in conjunction with high fertility rates, these demographic conditions ensured that an elastic supply of labor would continue in Brazil long after the cessation of massive immigration from abroad.

Both in the relative stagnation of per capita income during most of the nineteenth century, and in the onset of more rapid development toward the end of the period, Brazil showed some similarities with the well-known model of an economy caught in a low-income equilibrium trap.[11] This was not an economy in stasis, for aggregate economic expansion was occurring. Much of the increment in output, however, went to sustain a larger population rather than to provide higher per capita incomes for the population as a whole. As such, the economy resembled the quasi-stable equilibrium analyzed by Harvey Leibenstein and others, in which the forces tending to raise per capita incomes (e.g. export expansion, the opening of new lands) were largely offset by other conditions (such as population growth), which acted to restore per capita income to its previous level. In the Brazilian case, income distributional effects were also present because the endogenous adjustment mechanism operated mainly to reduce *labor* incomes. The wage-depressing force of population growth was especially potent because of the practice of importing low-cost, adult workers from overseas directly in response to changing conditions which raised the marginal value-product of labor. This rapid adjustment mechanism meant that the duration of disequilibrium states above the low-income level was brief.

The process through which Brazil broke out of this quasi-stable equilibrium and began a more generalized development pattern is also of interest. Here, too, the Brazilian experience resembled some aspects of the quasi-stable equilibrium model. A central feature of the model is that the onset of sustained development depends on discontinuities in which key variables spurt and increase at disproportionate rates. In the Brazilian case, the central non-linearity was the sharp increase in the supply of government expenditure and of foreign capital for infrastructure development which occurred in the last decades of the nineteenth century.[12]

We can now summarize briefly our answer to a question raised at the beginning of this study. Why did Brazil not develop economically during the nineteenth century along the lines of the United States, Australia, and other regions of recent settlement? It would be simplistic to expect a single-factor explanation for such a phenomenon; a number of conditions are pertinent.

Part of the answer relates to the especially poor economic experience of the Northeast during the nineteenth century. A large portion of Brazil's population lived in that region. Consequently, the Northeast's very low rate of economic development during the nineteenth century weighed heavily on the pace of the country's overall development. More generally, Brazil's elastic labor supply was a condition of basic importance in limiting economic development throughout this economy. The elastic supply of unskilled workers had adverse effects on capital formation, technical progress, and wage levels in Brazil. Nevertheless, Brazil's labor-market conditions did not constitute an all-determining barrier to the country's economic development. The experience of the Southeast suggests a qualifying perspective here. Once low-cost transportation became more widely available, the Southeast was able to achieve sustained economic development (albeit with a special pattern in wages and income distribution) despite the persistence of a highly elastic supply of labor. This experience also points to the strategic role of high transportation costs as an obstacle to Brazil's economic development.

This is not yet the end of the analytical chain. In principle, Brazil's interior could have been provided with roads or railways that much earlier in the century. The downward shift in agricultural supply curves that came with the provision of low-cost transportation could have occurred earlier in the century. Why was Brazil's interior not provided with railways (or better roads) much sooner? Public finance on a large scale would have been necessary to implement that infrastructure investment. And such a program was precluded by the state of Brazil's public finances. The public-finance constraint on development expenditure, in turn, stemmed from the conditions within Brazil's economy and policy which we discussed in Chapter 5.

Some Implications for Contemporary Developing Countries

Drawing lessons from an earlier historical experience is always a hazardous enterprise, for some key conditions have undoubtedly changed in the interim. But whether explicitly or in an implicit fashion, history is often examined for relevant pointers. And some features of Brazil's economic experience during the nineteenth century may indeed be relevant to contemporary less-developed countries as they frame their development strategies.

Most obviously, the Brazilian experience suggests that an absence of some often-cited barriers to development is not enough to generate rapid economic development. Ideological autonomy, microeconomic rationality, and an absence of imperialist domination provide important examples here. This historical case also suggests that the central problems for long-term economic development often involve aggregate supply rather than demand conditions. Brazil had loose fiscal and monetary policies and, relatedly, excess aggregate demand for several decades during the nineteenth century.[13] The result, however, was chronic inflation. Moreover, long-term inflation did not lead to generalized development in nineteenth-century Brazil. Buoyant aggregate demand was a necessary but not a sufficient condition for sustained development. The latter required the supply shifts which came with the expansion of the railways within Brazil's interior. Increased elasticity of supply meant that expansionary demand conditions could be transformed increasingly into sustained economic growth rather than mainly price inflation.

The Brazilian experience also attests to the possible usefulness of international trade as a source of income growth and economic development. Moreover, expanding primary-product exports were complementary rather than antithetical to a strategy of industrialization based on the domestic market. This historical case also makes plain that generalized economic development requires rising productivity in the domestic agricultural sector. (This observation would be platitudinous were it not that contemporary less-developed countries often implement policies which in effect discriminate against domestic agriculture.[14]) In addition, as we have seen, the role of government in providing public investment to generate external economies can be crucial for development in this sector. In the Brazilian case, investment in infrastructure to reduce internal transportation costs was of central importance. But the lessons concerning the importance of external economies for economic development also apply in more general terms.

Further, in contexts where external economies are prevalent, public finance takes on special significance for development. Because of the importance of public finance, competing concerns which consume limited government resources, for example, integrative activities or external political involvements, have a high opportunity cost. By the same token, political and fiscal decentralization may confer special advantages for economic development. Most importantly, decentralized constitutional arrangements may facilitate aggregate public-finance mobilization and the supply of public improvements at the sub-national level. A decentralization ('federal') strategy was not implemented in Brazil until late in the nineteenth century. In another respect, however, nineteenth-century Brazil was relatively fortunate. With the exception of the Paraguayan War, the country was virtually free of external involvements that would otherwise have made large claims on the limited public finance available. The contrast is with a situation like the pre-1914 Balkans, where regional balance-of-power considerations diverted considerable fiscal and administrative resources into military efforts.

Brazil's economic history also suggests some negative lessons. The country's low educational levels probably slowed the process of developing and diffusing improved techniques within agriculture. With the rate of technical progress a function of the stock of human capital, a country's small educational enrollments take on special significance. Moreover, because of rapid population growth, the percentage of illiterates in Brazil's population continued at a high level despite the large increases in enrollments.[15] This was only one of the ways in which high rates of labor-force growth were not consistent with generalized economic development in Brazil. Contemporary less-developed countries may find this case of special interest; for it was one in which rapid population increase took place in a country with abundant land. Throughout the century, unoccupied land within the interior remained plentiful in Brazil. Apparently this was not enough to offset the impact of rapid population growth on wage levels and the distribution of income. Because of high population growth, labor continued to be abundant (and cheap) relative to capital in Brazil, a condition with far-reaching economic (and social) consequences.

Finally, the economic history of the Northeast raises questions concerning the optimal size political and economic unit for economic development. As the experience of the Northeast indicates, being part of the largest and geographically most encompassing unit does not always confer net economic advantages.[16] The analytical perspective drawn from that experience may also help explain some cases of disparate regional development in contemporary developing countries. Such regional problems have often been analyzed in very different terms, but these have not always led to effective policy solutions. Further, the experience of the Northeast is also pertinent in the context of proposals for economic integration among existing less-developed countries. Brazil's economic experience provides a dramatic example of the unfortunate consequences when a condition stressed by the theory of optimum currency areas – factor mobility – is not satisfied. Under present conditions in some less-developed countries, effective factor reallocation may be limited not by migration costs (as in nineteenth-century Brazil), but by ethnic, tribal, or national hostilities.[17] But as we have seen, unless labor mobility is assured or economically equivalent measures are implemented to avoid currency-union effects such as afflicted the Northeast during the nineteenth century, the formation of larger political-economic units may not have a positive impact. Instead of generating the expected acceleration in overall development, creation of larger units may lead to the creation of regional backwaters and deadweight loss.[18]

The experience of the Northeast also suggests another lesson. The troubles which plagued the region stemmed from a basic underlying fact: the Northeast was part of a unit which violated the conditions which economic theory specifies for a currency union and a unified exchange rate. Thus, in a broader perspective, this experience indicates the real-world relevance of economic theory, and the real-world costs of policies which attempt to ignore it.

On some topics, this study has suggested new perspectives and the need for new interpretations of Brazil's economic past. For example, the underlying reasons for the Northeast's poor development experience in the nineteenth century is one instance where a new interpretation appears necessary. Our discussion of Brazil's government and its inadequate promotional activities during this period also revealed constraints both different and more compelling than may earlier have been appreciated. Finally, this study suggests the need for a more complex view of imperialism and dependency in Brazil since the middle of the nineteenth century. Some earlier accounts seem to have overstated the extent of Brazil's passivity and victimization at the hands of the metropolitan powers and the international economy.

As this discussion indicates, social science analysis can be useful in clarifying aspects of economic underdevelopment and development. Accordingly, the social scientist has a special responsibility in seeking a better understanding of these phenomena. Unfortunately, serious obstacles can stand in the way of fulfilling this truth-seeking role. Social or historical myths may have their own attractions. Preconceived notions and ideology can also distort the intellectual process. And whether the ideologies (and the attendant pressures for conformity) emanate from the broader society or from the academic community is immaterial in this context.[19] Such conditions may make more difficult, but do not render any less important, the role of the free social scientist.

Notes

1   These paragraphs draw on material which is presented in Nathaniel H. Leff, *Underdevelopment and Development in Brazil:* Vol. I *Economic Structure and Change, 1822–1947*, Chapter 7, pp. 144–9.
2   See pp. 82–3 in Chapter 4, above.
3   Ibid., pp. 101–3 in Chapter 5, above.
4   Data on this point are present in Leff, *Economic Structure and Change*, Chapter 7, n. 35, and Table 7.4. Our focus in the present context is on the total stock of foreign investment on Brazilian infrastructure. Hence the relevant data in the table just cited are the aggregate rather than the per capita figures.
5   The material underlying this statement is presented in Chapter 4, above.
6   See Leff, *Economic Structure and Change,* op. cit., Chapter 5, pp. 87–93.
7   See pp. 20–7 in Chapter 2, above.
8   For a formal analysis of the situation confronting landowners in land-rich countries, and a discussion of their institutional responses in other historical contexts, see Evsey Domar, 'The Causes of Slavery or Serfdom: A Hypothesis,' *Journal of Economic History*, vol. 30 (March 1970).
9   On this question, see pp. 66–7 in Chapter 4 of Leff, *Economic Structure and Change*, op. cit.
10 Nathaniel H. Leff and Herbert S. Klein, 'O Crescimento da População Não-Européia antes do Início do Desenvolvimento: O Brasil do Século XIX,' *Anais de História*, vol. 6 (1974); and Thomas Merrick and Douglas Graham, *Population and Economic Development in Brazil, 1800 to the Present* (Baltimore: Johns Hopkins University Press, 1979), Chapter 3.
11 See, for example, Harvey Leibenstein, *Economic Backwardness and Economic Growth* (New York: Wiley, 1957), esp. Chapters 3 and 8; and Richard R. Nelson,

'A Theory of the Low-Level Equilibrium Trap in Underdeveloped Economies,' *American Economic Review* (December 1956).

12 See pp. 144–53 in Leff, *Economic Structure and Change*, Chapter 7. In some respects, the discontinuities mentioned in the text approximate analytical features of the process discussed by W. W. Rostow in his 'The Take-Off into Self-Sustained Economic Growth,' *Economic Journal*, vol. 66 (March 1956).

13 On the points which follow in this paragraph, see Chapter 6 of Leff, *Economic Structure and Change*.

14 See, for example, Michael Lipton, *Why Poor People Stay Poor: Urban Bias in World Development* (Cambridge, Mass.: Harvard University Press, 1978).

15 See pp. 18–20 in Chapter 2 of Leff, *Economic Structure and Change*.

16 See pp. 21–30 in Chapter 2, above. For the reasons discussed there, the pace of export growth and development in the Northeast would have been greater in the nineteenth century if the region had been an independent political-economic unit. But as indicated in Chapter 2 the optimal size political unit is not decided on narrow economic grounds alone.

17 Examples of cases in which such hostilities have restricted labor mobility are the massacre of Ibos in Northern Nigeria before the Biafran War, and the 1969 war between two members of the Central American Common Market, El Salvador and Honduras. Note that the analytical literature on economic integration between developing countries usually assumes away the question of geographical and inter-activity factor mobility. But unless these problems are resolved, the gains which accrue from the topics which are discussed (e.g. trade creation and coordinated investment policy) may be vastly overshadowed by losses due to factor immobility – the omitted item in the discussion.

18 In many developing countries, hostilities of the sort mentioned in the previous note may restrict serious efforts at economic integration between existing countries. However, the analysis presented in the text is also relevant for another issue which confronts some contemporary developing countries: assessing the potential costs and benefits which may accrue from fragmentation of existing political and monetary units.

19 Some comments by Barrington Moore, Jr, are relevant here: 'Furthermore the denial that objective truth is possible in principle flings open the door to the worst forms of intellectual dishonesty. A crude version goes something like this: since neutrality is impossible I will take my stand with the underdog and write history to serve the underdog, helping in this way to reach a "higher Truth". In plain language that is just cheating.' This quotation is from Barrington Moore, Jr, *Social Origins of Dictatorship and Democracy* (Boston: Beacon Press, 1966), p. 522.

Index

Page numbers in italics refer to tables.